**HEATH
SCIENCE
SERIES**

Illustrated by R O B E R T M A C L E A N and Elaine Wentworth,
Cynthia and Alvin Koehler

SCIENCE

FAR AND NEAR
SECOND EDITION

By Herman and Nina Schneider

BOOK THREE

D. C. HEATH AND COMPANY BOSTON

CONTENTS

Here you are, reading a book! It is a book about science, and people used science in making the book. By using science, they found out how to make this smooth, white paper out of rough, dark trees.

Because people use science, you have better clothes to wear, more kinds of food to enjoy, and better homes to live in than the people of long ago.

You can travel more quickly on land, on sea, and in the air. Some day you may even travel through space to the moon and beyond.

OFF TO THE MOON

Some day it may happen.

It may happen before you are grown up!

A rocket ship with people will be sent to the moon. The people will find out many things that we do not yet know.

Of course, we already know some things about the moon. We know it is a ball like the earth, but smaller.

The moon does not shine with its own light. Like the earth, it is lit up by the bright sun.

The moon travels around the earth. The moon takes about a month to go around the earth. We know that as the moon travels around the earth it seems to change shape.

Ready! Aim! Where?

Let's pretend that everything is ready. The scientists are ready to aim the moon rocket. Should they aim it at the moon?

No! If they aim the rocket at the moon, it will never get there. Scientists say they will aim it somewhere else. Where?

And why? You can do an experiment to find out where to aim.

EXPERIMENT

You will need a large ball, a piece of chalk, and a helper. You will be the earth, your helper will be the moon, and the ball will be the rocket ship.

Draw a large circle on the floor. You (the earth) stand in the center of the circle. The moon person stands on the circle. The circle is the path of the moon as it moves around the earth.

Now the moon starts to walk quickly along its path. Now you are ready to send your ball rocket to the moon! As the moon comes in front of you, roll the ball at him. Did you hit the moon? No! Not if you aimed right at him.

You aimed the ball to the place where you saw the moon. But while the ball was rolling the moon was moving. When the ball reached the path of the moon, the moon had already moved on to a new place.

So, if you want the ball rocket to hit the moon, you should not aim it at the moon. Should you aim it in front or behind? Why?

How much ahead of the moon should you aim the ball rocket? You could try again and again until you got it right. You could use the same ball again and again.

But a real rocket cannot be used again and again. Also, a real rocket costs a lot of money. So the scientists must try to aim the rocket right the first time. To aim it right they must know many things. Three things are very important. Try to guess what these three things are before you read ahead. It will help you if you do the experiment again while you try to guess.

The three things are:
1. How fast is the rocket ball going?
2. How fast is the moon going?
3. How far is the moon from the earth?

For your experiment the answers are small numbers. Your rocket ball is not going very fast. Your moon friend is not going very fast, and he is not far away. But a real rocket goes very fast, and so does the moon. Also the moon is very far away. So the numbers for a real rocket trip will be quite large. Here they are:

1. A rocket ship to the moon will travel about 25,000 miles an hour at top speed. After a while, it will begin to slow down.

2. The moon travels more than 2,000 miles an hour.

3. The moon is about 240,000 miles from the earth.

What nice large numbers! It would take many years to do all the arithmetic for one trip to the moon. But we don't have to. This machine can do all that arithmetic in a few minutes!

How would you like to have such a machine to use in your next arithmetic test?

Almost There

When the moon travelers are almost there, what will they see? Will everything seem strange and new to them?

No, not everything. The travelers will already know many things about the moon. They will know because scientists have studied the moon for hundreds of years.

First they studied the moon through small telescopes. Then they made bigger and better telescopes. With these they took big pictures of the moon. They used the telescopes to find out many interesting things about the land of the moon.

But scientists want to know more and more. They send rockets far out into space. They aim some of these rockets to travel around the earth like little moons. They aim some to reach the moon. With these rockets they find out about the air around the earth. They also find out about the space between the earth and the moon.

Have any rockets landed on the moon? Tell what you know about moon travel today.

On the Moon

When the travelers land, what will they see? Scientists think that the moon will look something like this. Mountains of rock, rock and dust, not a drop of water, not one living thing — this is what they think they will find.

The travelers must be careful not to touch anything with their bare hands. The sunlit rocks are hotter than boiling water. The shady places are much colder than a freezer. This is because the moon has no air. Air on the earth is like a thick soft blanket. It keeps the sun from making the earth too hot. It keeps the shady places from becoming too cold.

Let's go back home, back to the earth!

The Moon's Changing Shape

Sometimes the moon looks like a whole circle. Sometimes the moon looks like a half circle. Other times the moon looks like a slice of lemon peel.

Why does the moon change its shape all the time? You can find out by doing this experiment.

EXPERIMENT

You will need an electric light, a ball, a few sheets of black paper, and a piece of white chalk.

In this experiment the ball will be the moon. The electric light will be the sun. You will be the earth.

In this experiment you will make the moon travel around you. The real moon travels, too. It travels around the real earth.

You will use the electric light to shine on the little moon. The real moon has light shining on it, too. The light shines from the sun.

Sit with the light behind you.

Hold the ball in front of you, a little higher than your head. See the sun shining on the moon. Make a picture of what you see, with white chalk on black paper. Does the picture look like this?

The picture shows a full circle. When we see the real moon like this, we call it a full moon. At full moon you can see all of the lit-up side of the moon. The other side is in the dark, but you cannot see the dark side. It is not facing the earth.

Now let's make the little moon travel like the real moon.

To do this, move the ball to the left, slowly. See what happens. The sun is still shining on the moon. The moon still has a lit-up side and a dark side. But what do you see?

You do not see a full circle of lit-up moon. You see a part of the lit-up side and a part of the dark side. Make a picture of it. Does it look something like this?

When we see half of the lit-up side of the moon, we call it a half moon.

Keep the little moon travel-ing in the sunlight. Soon you will see the moon like this.

It looks this way because you see only a little of the lit-up side. You see a lot of the dark side.

Keep the little moon traveling. Soon you will see more and more of the lit-up side.

You will see this.

Then you will see this.

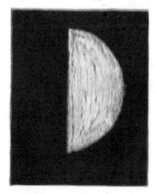

Then you will see this.

As you start around
again you will see less and less of the lit-up side.

Now you know about the changing shape of the moon. It seems to change as the moon travels around the earth. As it travels, we see less and less of the lit-up side. Then we see more and more.

Over and over again, we see these changes of the moon. It takes about four weeks for the moon to travel through all the changes.

Venus
Mars
Saturn
Neptune

Mercury
Earth
Jupiter
Uranus
Pluto

Off to the Planets

After the first few trips to the moon, scientists will plan trips to the planets. We are already on one of the planets. The other planets are like the earth in some ways. They are large and round. As you can see in the picture, all the planets also travel on paths around the sun. They get light and heat from the sun, too. There are nine planets in all. Four are larger than the earth. Four are smaller than the earth.

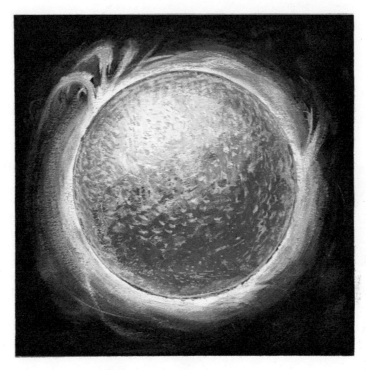

Off to the Stars

First to the moon and then to the planets. Will we ever travel to the stars? If so, would you like to go? These facts may help you to decide.

Stars are huge hot suns. They are much hotter than the hottest flame you have ever seen. They are much larger than the earth. Many of them are larger and hotter than the sun. Like the sun, they shine with a bright light all the time, night and day.

Night and day? Then why don't we see any stars in the daytime? What happens to them? Let's find out.

EXPERIMENT

Get a small flashlight or electric light. Darken the room. Now turn the small light on and off. You will notice something. In a darkened room the light seems quite bright.

Now let up the shade and hold the flashlight in front of the window.

Look at the small light as you turn it on and off. Can you see the light against the bright sky?

The light from the flashlight does not seem very bright, even though the flashlight gives the same light in the dark room and in the light room. It is the same flashlight whether the shades are up or down.

In the same way, the stars seem bright at night, when you see them shining in a dark sky.

In the daytime the sky is brightly lit up by the sun. You cannot see the stars against the bright sky.

EXPERIMENT

You can make the stars seem to disappear. On a starry night place a lamp on the window sill. Then turn out all the lights in the room. Look out the window and see how many stars you can count right in front of you.

Now turn on the lamp. How many stars can you count now? The light from your lamp made many of the stars seem to disappear. The much brighter light of the sun makes all the stars seem to disappear during the day.

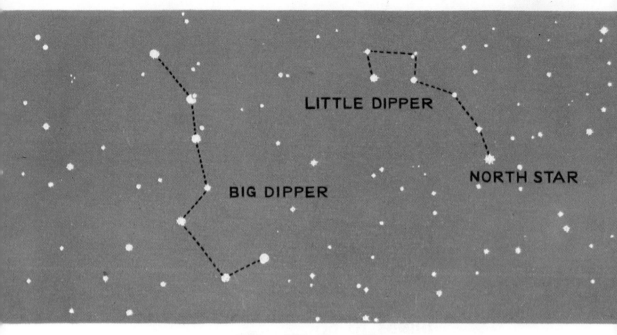

LITTLE DIPPER

BIG DIPPER

NORTH STAR

The Night Sky

You can see thousands of stars in the sky. If you look carefully, you can begin to know some of the star groups.

Some star groups are shown in the picture on this page. Look at them. Then look at the sky tonight. Can you find the Big Dipper? the Little Dipper? and the North Star?

The sky near your home may not look just like the picture on this page. The way the sky looks at night depends on what time of year it is and in what part of the world you are. How would dusty or smoky air make a difference in the way the sky looks? And how would bright street lights make a difference?

THINGS TO TALK ABOUT

1. Talk about taking a trip to the moon. How would you get there? What would you wear? What would you find there?

2. Tell how sunlight is different from moon-light.

3. Read Indian stories about the moon and stars. Tell them to your class.

4. Talk about the animals that have been sent by rocket into space. What did we learn from the trips these animals took?

THINGS TO DO

1. Look for the first star that comes out in the evening sky. How long does it take before you see the second star?

2. Make a book about space travel. Get pictures and newspaper stories about the trips made into space.

3. With two other children in your class act out the travels of the earth and the moon around the sun.

4. Watch the moon each night for a month. Watch it from the same place and at about the same time. Make drawings of what you see. Write the date and time on each picture.

5. Learn more about the star groups. Make pictures of them. Use blue paper and gold or silver stars to show the different star groups. Tell how each group got its name.

THINGS TO FIND OUT

1. Find out the names of the planets that travel around the sun. Learn how the planets are different from each other.

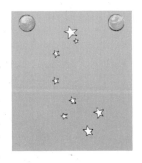

2. Find out why you can sometimes see the moon during the day.

3. Find out why the North Star is such an important star. Where is it in the sky? Look for it.

4. Find out why the star groups do not always appear in the same place in the sky.

5. Find out what tools are used to study the sky and to learn more about space. Try to find pictures of these tools.

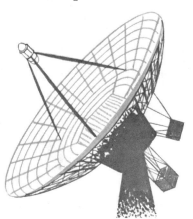

THE EARTH'S COVER

Dig, dig, dig to China. A whole afternoon of digging, and no China yet! Has anyone ever told you that if you dig deep enough, you will find yourself in China?

Perhaps you tried, and all you found was sand and still more sand.

If you could dig deep enough, what do you think you would find?

Solid rock! Dig deep enough and you come to solid rock. Dig anywhere, under the fields, under the city, even under the sea. You will always come to rock. You live on a world of hard, strong rock.

Rock in Soil

Of course, you do not live right on the rock. In most places there is soft soil between you and the rock of the world.

In this soft soil grow most of the green plants of the world. Green plants make the food that living things need.

Most plants grow in soil. Most soil has rock in it, as you can see from this experiment.

EXPERIMENT

Put some soil into a jar of water. Let it stand for a while.

Then slowly pour off the water and the soil that did not sink.

Take some soil from the bottom of the jar. Feel it. You can feel and see that the soil at the bottom of the jar has small pieces of rock in it.

Perhaps you will say, "These are not pieces of rock! These are just pebbles and sand."

But the pebbles and sand were once part of huge mountains of rock.

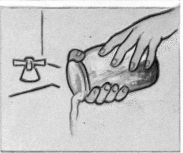

Huge mountains of hard rock were broken into tiny bits, into pebbles and sand, and into soft, fine soil.

What hammers are strong enough to break huge mountains into tiny bits?

The hammers are sunlight, water, and plants. These things, softer than a feather, can break the hardest rock. Working slowly, for millions of years, they turn the rock into soil.

Let's find out a little about how rock can be changed to soil.

Heat and Rock

Here is a mountain being broken to bits by sunlight. Of course, you cannot see it breaking up. It would take millions of years for sunlight alone to break up a mountain. Shining and shining day after day, year after year, the sun heats the rock. And night after night the rock cools. Year in and year out, the rock is heated and cooled, heated and cooled, heated and cooled.

After a long, long time a piece of the rock splits away. A little at a time, over millions of years, the mountain is broken into small pieces that become part of the soil.

Perhaps you have seen other things broken by heat. Sometimes a cold drinking glass cracks when very hot water is poured into it.

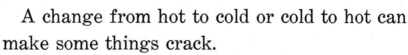

Sometimes a warm glass breaks when cold water is poured into it.

A change from hot to cold or cold to hot can make some things crack.

How can heat make things break apart? Here is a way to find out.

EXPERIMENT

Get a clean empty jar with a screw cover. Screw the cover on so tightly that it is too hard for you to open.

Then run hot water over the cover.

Dry it off. Now try to open it. Is it easier now?

Why did the cover come off easily? Because the cover became bigger. The heat of the hot water made it bigger.

Most things become bigger when they are heated. We say they expand.

When hot water is poured into a cold drinking glass, the inside of the glass gets hot and expands more quickly than the outside. This makes a break in the glass.

Some things are built with room to expand with heat. Concrete sidewalks have cracks built into them. On a hot day concrete sidewalks can expand without breaking.

Train tracks, too, are laid with a little space between the pieces of track. In the hot sunlight the tracks get a little bigger. The tracks can expand without breaking.

Stones around a campfire are sometimes broken by heat. Each stone is heated more on the side near the fire. This side expands more, until finally it cracks or breaks off.

You may have seen some stones that have been broken like this.

In the same way, the heat of the sun can break rocks. The sun's heat works much more slowly than fire. That is why you cannot see rocks breaking apart in the sunlight. But over many years, the sun heats the rocks. The outside of the rock heats more than the inside. The outside expands more, and after many years the outside begins to crack until finally it breaks off.

A bit here and a piece there, the mountains are split and crumbled.

Water and Rock

Mountains never seem to change, but they do. A great changer is water. Water can slowly cut down the highest, hardest mountain.

Every little stream, every brook, every river, works like a saw cutting away at the rock underneath.

The water carries along grains of sand and bits of pebbles and stones that scratch and cut at the rock.

In times of heavy rains a river rushes fast. Big rocks are rolled along. They bang and smash as they go. Pebbles click and clatter against each other and against the rock of the river bed. The sand is rushed along, scratching and rubbing as it goes.

A bit at a time, a grain here and a pebble there, the flowing water cuts deeper and deeper into its bed.

Over millions of years the mountain rock is cut apart into stones, pebbles, and fine sand, and carried down by flowing water.

The water slows down as it reaches flatter land. What happens when the water does not rush so quickly?

EXPERIMENT

Shake a jar of soil and water.

See how the soil is kept up and moved around when the water moves quickly.

Now stop shaking the jar. See how the soil begins to sink as the water begins to slow down.

The same thing happens when water flows across the land. When the water flows fast, it carries along bits of rock.

When the water slows down, the bits of rock are dropped. Bits of mountain become part of the soil.

Ice and Rock

Water breaks rock in another way, too. You know that when water becomes very cold it freezes. It turns to ice.

Something strange happens when water changes to ice. It becomes bigger. The ice takes up more room than the water.

You can see this for yourself.

E X P E R I M E N T

Fill an empty ice tray with water. Fill it to the top of the tray.

Let the water freeze. Now look at it.

The ice is heaped up higher than the top of the tray. When the water changes to ice it becomes bigger. It takes up more room.

As water freezes and gets bigger, it can push very hard. Here is an experiment that shows how hard it can push.

EXPERIMENT

Fill a bottle with water, right to the top, and leave another bottle of the same size empty.

Put the covers of both bottles on very tightly. Then put both bottles into paper bags and close the tops of the bags.

Place the paper bags in a very cold place. Leave them there until the water freezes.

Then take out the paper bags and look inside. Did anything happen to the empty bottle? What happened to the bottle with water? What made it happen? Why was an empty bottle also used in this experiment?

You saw that freezing water can break glass. It can also break rocks. When water flows into a crack in a rock and then freezes to ice, it becomes bigger.

The ice pushes against the sides of the rock and splits it apart.

Year after year, a little at a time, mountains of rock are broken apart by freezing water.

Plants and Rock

Have you ever seen these plants growing on rock?

You know that most plants grow in soil. Where is the soil for these plants?

These plants help to make soil out of the rock. They soften the rock until it crumbles a little. If you pick off a piece of the plant you can see bits of soft, crumbly rock underneath.

This is rock being turned to soil by the plants that grow on it.

Plants, water, and sunshine all help to make soil out of rock. As the rock is crumbled to bits, other plants can grow in it.

All soils have crumbled rock in them. Most soils have crumbled plants in them, too. Sunshine and water, as well as plants, all help to make soil out of rock.

There are many kinds of plants and many kinds of rocks. Do you think there are many kinds of soils, too? Here is how you can find out for yourself.

EXPERIMENT

Bring in soil from different places. Try to get some from a farm, some from the woods, some from near a brook or river, or from other different places.

Put cupfuls of the soils into jars of water. Let the jars stand until the water is almost clear.

Now look at the different soils. Do they all look alike?

Are they all of the same color?

The rock material sank to the bottom. Does each cupful of soil have the same amount of rock material?

Most of the plant material is lighter than water and has floated to the top. Does each cupful of soil have the same amount of plant material?

In what ways are the soils different?

THINGS TO TALK ABOUT

1. Talk about ways the farmer can help save the soil.

2. Tell why most pebbles are round and smooth.

3. Have you ever seen a bottle of milk look like this? What happened to it?

4. Tell how plants, water, and sun can wear away the land.

5. Tell why good soil is so important to us.

THINGS TO DO

1. Get a piece of wire screen. Put some soil on it. Shake the screen back and forth over a piece of newspaper. See what falls through the screen onto the newspaper. See if any small pieces of rock are left on the screen.

2. Go to a road cut or to a place where a cellar is being dug. Look at the plants and the soil at the top. Is the soil at the top a different color from the soil down below?

3. Find out what is living in the soil. Dig up some soil from your garden. Four inches is usually far enough to find something interesting. Bring the soil inside. Put the soil on a sheet of white paper. Spread the soil around. What do you find?

40

4. Look for large rocks with cracks in them. Are there any plants growing in the cracks? Can you find a cracked rock that has a tree growing on it?

5. What happens to bare soil in the rain? To find out spread some soil on a board like this. Put a pan at the lower end. Sprinkle water at the higher end. What part of the soil washes down into the pan? Is it the soft, dark material or is it the pebbles and sand?

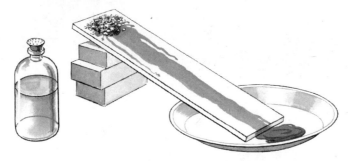

THINGS TO FIND OUT

1. Find out how plants and animals make the soil better for plants to grow in.

2. These words are important to the farmer and the gardener. Find out what they mean and then tell why they are important: rich, moist soil; coarse sand; sandy loam; humus; well-drained soil; gravelly soil; clay soil; loam.

3. Find out what kinds of plants can grow on rocks. Look for some of these plants.

DESERT PLANTS AND ANIMALS

Have you ever visited a desert in summer? If you have, you know how hot it is in the daytime. You know how the sun beats down upon the hot, dry desert.

How can anything live in the desert? The land is almost too hot to touch. Months go by without a drop of rain. How can anything live?

But plants and animals do live in the desert. Perhaps they have special ways that help them to live there. Let's see!

Animals in the Desert

In the desert there are animals that hide in the shade or stay quiet in the hot sunlight. You have to look sharply to see them. Let's look sharply for some of the animals that live in and near the hot, dry desert.

Here is a desert snake. It can curl itself into the shade between two rocks. It may stay there a long time waiting for its meal. Perhaps a desert mouse or a bird will come along. Then zip, and it's lunch time!

The desert snake won't need supper that night because it can get along for many days without eating.

A desert is a good place for desert snakes to be born. Some kinds of desert snakes are born alive and some hatch from eggs. Here are some baby desert snakes hatching from eggs. The mother snake laid the eggs in the warm sand. The sand kept the eggs warm. Now the baby snakes are ready and they hatch out.

A snake's skin is the right skin for a desert animal. It is hard, like your fingernail. The next experiment will show how this helps.

Rub your fingernail on some rough sand or sandpaper. Then rub your finger tip across the sand or sandpaper.

A snake's skin is hard like your fingernail. When the snake crawls along, the sand and rocks do not hurt its hard skin.

A desert snake's skin helps in other ways. It is made of thick scales which help keep the snake from drying up in the hot sun. The scales also help it to move by pushing against the ground.

What would happen if a snake had a smooth skin without scales? What happened when you wore your smooth new shoes the first time? Did you slide? A snake with a smooth skin and no scales could not move quickly. It would slip and slide.

Snakes are built right for being snakes. Desert snakes are built right for living in the hot, sandy desert.

This fat little animal often lives near the desert. It is called a prairie dog. Prairie dogs like to live together in deep tunnels. With their strong feet and sharp claws they dig deep, deep underground. There the prairie-dog families are safe from harm.

In its tunnel a prairie dog can hide from anything that likes to eat fat little animals. And it can hide from something else, too. You can find out what that is by making a tunnel yourself.

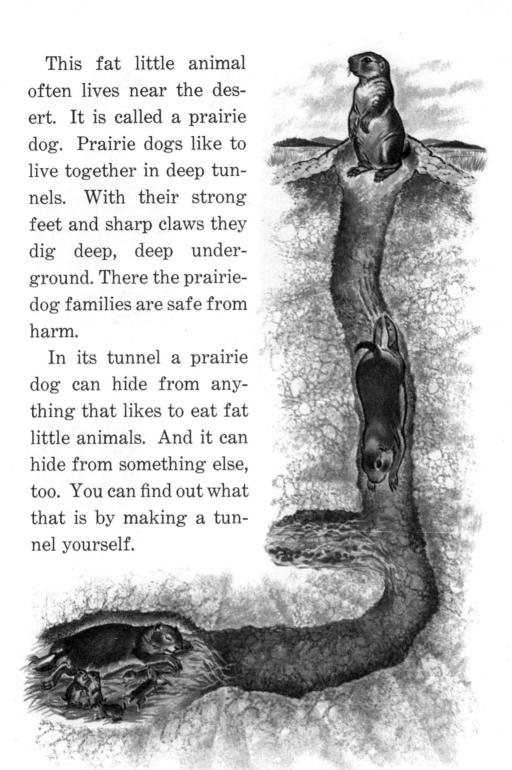

You cannot make a real prairie-dog tunnel in the classroom. But you can make a little tunnel and do an experiment with it.

EXPERIMENT

Get a flowerpot full of dry earth. Make a deep hole with a stick. That is your tunnel.

Then put the pot out in the sun for a while.

Feel the earth on top of the pot. Then put your finger into the hole. Which feels cooler? Now try it with a thermometer. Why is a deep tunnel a good home for a prairie dog who lives where it is hot and dry most of the time?

In their cool tunnels the prairie dogs nibble at the seeds, grass, and roots they bring down. When they do go up, one of the prairie dogs watches, while the others are busy looking for food or playing.

If the watcher sees trouble, it barks. Once, twice, and zip, down go the prairie dogs into the safe tunnel homes that they built together. Prairie dogs always live together in villages. Sometimes these villages are very large and may contain more than a thousand prairie dogs.

Because prairie dogs work together and help each other, they can often get away from other animals that would like to eat them.

A Desert Bird

This desert bird is a road runner. It is not
the most beautiful bird in the world, but it
does not need to be beautiful. It is quick
enough and clever enough to fight a big snake.
It can kill it and eat it. A road runner likes
lizards, too. With its long sharp beak a road
runner can reach right into a crack in a rock.
Its long claws are built right for running on
the desert sand.

A road runner is right for the desert!

Cactus, a Desert Plant

Here is a plant whose ways are just right for the hot, dry desert. Round and fat with a thick skin, it looks like a barrel. And it is a kind of barrel, but not an empty one. Inside it is soft and full of water like a watermelon.

The cactus can save its water for a long time. Its shape helps the plant save water. How? You can do an experiment to find out.

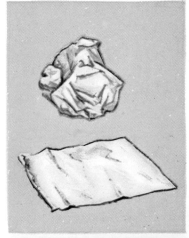

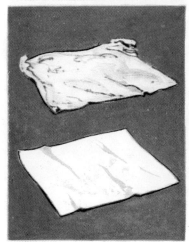

EXPERIMENT

Cut two narrow strips of paper. Wet both of them.

Crumple one of the pieces into a round ball. Leave the other piece straight and flat.

Put both pieces in a warm place, and wait for them to dry. Which takes longer?

Now can you tell why a round, fat shape is a very good shape for saving water?

Would thin, flat leaves be as good for a desert plant?

A fat shape, soft and full of water like a watermelon — that is fine for desert plants. But it is also fine for hungry, thirsty desert animals. Why don't animals eat them?

Animals don't eat such plants for the same reason that you would not care to eat a hairbrush. Just look at those sharp points! They are too sharp for even a very thirsty animal.

Many desert plants have sharp points that keep off hungry animals. And they also have thick skins and round shapes or thick leaves that save water. Some of these desert plants have still another desert way that you do not see so easily.

Their long shallow roots spread out under the desert and take water from all around. A desert plant is right for the desert.

Plants and animals that live in the desert have special desert ways. But how can people live here? Here is a place of rocks, sand, and very little water. It is hard to live here. It is a place for special desert ways. People have special ways for living in the desert, too.

People have found special ways to live in hot, dry places and in hot, wet places. They have found ways to live in snow-covered lands and in lands where it never snows. People can learn to live in many different kinds of places.

People can think. They can find out new ways. They can share with each other what they find out. Because they can think, and share what they find out, people can live in many different places.

THINGS TO TALK ABOUT

1. Talk about how a desert is different from where you live.

2. Talk about how the Indians who lived in the desert got their food.

3. Talk about why so many of the desert animals are quiet during the day but move around at night.

THINGS TO DO

1. Make a desert garden in a bowl. What kind of soil would you put in it? What kinds of plants would you put in it? How often would you water them?

2. Look at a map of our country. Where are the deserts? Make a map of the country. Color the deserts yellow and the rest of the country green.

3. Cut out or draw pictures of animals that live in the desert. Make a book of them. Make a book of plants that live in the desert.

4. Make a desert word book. Find out what the words mesa, arroyo, badlands, mesquite, and yucca mean. Write what these words mean in your book. Draw or cut out pictures of these things. Put them in your book, too.

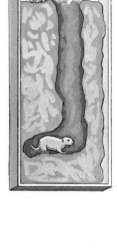

5. Use a thermometer on a sunny day to find out how much warmer it is in the sunshine than in the shade.

6. Make a small prairie-dog tunnel with clay.

THINGS TO FIND OUT

1. Find out what trees can live in a desert. How are they different from the trees that live in your neighborhood?

2. Find out how desert animals use color changes to keep themselves safe.

3. Find out how a hen warms up its eggs. Why can't a snake warm its eggs the same way?

4. Find out what animals make tunnels under the ground.

5. Find out in which deserts this animal lives. Why is it such a useful animal?

WE USE ROCK AND CLAY

If you went to live in the desert you would need a home. In the desert there are very few trees to give wood for building homes. What else could you find?

Long ago the Indians who came to the desert found plenty of rock all around. Could they use rock for building homes? Yes, they could if they could find some way of breaking it or cutting it into blocks.

The Indians found such a way. They found that some rocks are much harder than others. They made tools out of hard rock. With these hard rock tools they broke the softer rock. They broke it into blocks.

It was hard work, but they worked together and built big, cool houses. They made homes of soft rock that they cut with tools of hard rock.

There are many kinds of rock. Some are much harder than others. The very hard kinds can be used in some ways. The softer kinds are easier to cut into blocks.

Here are rocks being used in different ways. Tell which you think is hard rock. Which do you think is softer?

Testing Rock

When you hit a rock with your toe, any rock feels hard. How can you tell which rocks are harder than others? Here is one way to test the hardness of rocks.

EXPERIMENT

Bring some rocks to school. Choose two of them. Try to scratch one rock with another. The one that makes a scratch mark is harder. The softer rock will not scratch the harder rock.

After you have tried them all, you can lay the rocks in line. Put the softest at one end and the hardest at the other.

There are many different kinds of rock. One way of telling them apart is by their hardness.

Now look at the rocks. Do some of them seem to be made of grains of sand that were stuck together?

Rub two of these pieces together. Do grains of sand rub off?

Sandstone

Some rocks are really made of sand. Rock that is made of grains of sand stuck together is called sandstone. These pieces of sandstone were made millions of years ago.

Millions of years ago there was a huge sea that covered a large part of this country. Rivers flowed into this sea, bringing in sand that sank slowly to the bottom.

More and more sand flowed in and sank down. It heaped up higher and higher, heavier and heavier. The heavy heaps squeezed down on the sand below.

You know what happens when you squeeze a ball of wet sand. Try it.

The wet sand sticks together.

The same thing happened to the sand in the sea. It stuck together. In the sea water there were materials that stuck the sand together and made it into stone.

After millions of years, the loose sand at the bottom of the sea was changed to sandstone. Still later, the sea dried away and left the sandstone. Thick layers of it covered a large part of this country.

Indians used sandstone for building their homes in the desert. People still use it today. You may have seen city houses with front steps and walls made of sandstone.

What a long way that sandstone has traveled! Perhaps it was once part of a mountain. Before that, it was at the bottom of the sea. Now it is part of a city house.

Clay

The Indians found clay in the desert and canyon country. They saw that when clay is mixed with water it becomes soft and can be made into many shapes. Then, when the wet clay is dried, it becomes hard.

The Indians made many useful things out of clay. They made pots and bowls. They made clay toys and dolls. They made a kind of brick for building houses. It is called adobe brick. In some places adobe brick is still used for building houses.

Bricks of Clay

Here is how you can make adobe bricks.

EXPERIMENT

Mix clay with cut-up straw and water. Pour this material into a milk carton you have cut down.

Leave the carton in the sun for a day or two.

Then take out your brick and finish drying it.

Clay for Pots

Clay is good for making pots, and pots are good for storing things. The Indians stored nuts and seeds and other dry foods in the clay pots they made. But when they tried to use the pots for storing water, they found that water does something to the clay. You can find out what it does.

EXPERIMENT

Put a piece of dry clay in water and let it stay for a while. Stir the water and look at it. Is the water clear or cloudy? What do you think made it that way? Take out the piece of clay and feel it. Is it as hard as dry clay, or is it soft and crumbly?

Water makes clay soft. That is why the Indians could not store water in their clay pots.

There is a way of changing clay so that it does not become soft and crumbly.

In many parts of the world people have found the way.

They use heat.

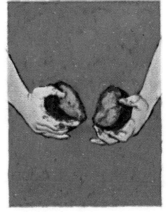

67

Heat Changes Clay

EXPERIMENT

Get a piece of a broken clay flowerpot and some pieces of broken dishes. Put the pieces in some water. Leave them there for a while and then stir the water. Does the water become cloudy?

What kept these pieces of clay from becoming soft and crumbly in the water?

Baking! Clay dishes are baked in big hot ovens, called kilns. When clay is heated very, very hot, it is changed. It becomes harder and stronger. Heat can change many things.

Perhaps there is a kiln in your school. A kiln can be used for baking the clay things that you can make.

The clay things are put into the kiln. The door is shut. Then the heat is turned on for a while. The heat comes from an electric heater or from a gas flame. The clay things are baked and become harder and stronger.

Dishes Today

Today, the dishes we use are not made slowly by hand. Scientists have helped to make many machines that make dishes quickly and cheaply. Because dishes are made so quickly and cheaply, many people can have them.

Look at the bottoms of some dishes and cups. You will find that dishes are made in many parts of the world.

Bring in some pieces of broken china, flowerpots, and other clay things. Look at the broken edges.

You will see there are many kinds and colors of clay. When the grains of clay are very small, we can make very smooth, thin dishes. Clay with larger grains is used for flowerpots, bricks, and other things that do not have to be smooth.

Clay Every Day

You use things made of baked clay every day. You eat out of clay dishes. The plants on the window sill grow in baked clay pots. Perhaps your school is made of baked clay bricks.

All these things, and many more, are made in very large kilns. These kilns can bake thousands of bricks or dishes at one time.

How long does it take you to make a clay dish? Just think how long it would take to make a set of dishes for your family! Think how long it would take to make dishes for all the children who eat in the lunchroom!

Where Does Clay Come From?

All clay is made of certain kinds of rocks. The rocks were slowly broken into tiny grains by sunlight, water, and plants. The grains were carried away by water. In some places they piled up in heaps called clay beds.

Clay comes from rocks of different colors, so we find clay in different colors, too.

Today people dig up the different kinds of clay to make bricks, dishes, and other useful things. Perhaps you ate breakfast on a plate that was part of a mountain millions of years ago.

THINGS TO TALK ABOUT

1. Talk about the things you have made from sand or clay.

2. Talk about the ways rock can be used.

3. Talk about why adobe houses are built only where there is very little rain.

4. Talk about things made of clay in your home and school.

5. Talk about some things that are changed when they are heated.

THINGS TO DO

1. Make a collection of rocks that have different colors.

2. Look at buildings made of brick. Are all bricks the same color? Make drawings to show the ways in which bricks are placed in a wall.

3. Take a walk in your neighborhood to find houses that are built of rock. What parts of your house are made of rock?

4. Find some colored pictures of the Grand Canyon. Look at the layers of colored sandstone and other rock.

THINGS TO FIND OUT

1. Find out how the Indians made arrowheads of rock. What other tools did the Indians make from rock?

2. Find out how sandstone is cut into pieces which can be used for building.

3. Find out where dishes are made in our country.

4. Find out how many different things in your school are made out of materials that were dug out of the earth.

5. Find out what these words mean: china, porcelain, glaze, ceramic, quarry.

6. Find out what kind of rock is found in your state. Can any of it be used for building?

WATER FOR FARMS AND HOMES

Wherever people live they must have food. The Indians of the desert knew how to grow plants that are good to eat.

Plants need soil and sunlight, and there is plenty of both in the desert. But plants also need water, and it almost never rains in the desert.

Could plants get their water in another way than from rain falling on them? Do plants get water through their roots? We can find out.

How Plants Get Water

EXPERIMENT

Get two plants of the same kind and size. Cover the soil around one plant with wax paper. Sprinkle water on the leaves of this plant. Sprinkle water on the soil of the other plant. Do this every day. Then see what happens. Which plant grows well? Which plant begins to dry up and die?

The plant that gets water only on the leaves does not grow well. Soon it dries up because the plant does not get enough water through its leaves.

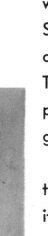

Plants get water through the roots in the soil. So you see, plants need water in the soil. When it rains, water gets into the soil. Are there other ways for water to get into the soil?

Ditches for Water

Although it almost never rains in the desert, the Indians found a way to get water for their farms. They dug ditches from the river to their farms. The water flowed through the ditches into the farm soil.

Soon the Indians wanted bigger farms. But the ditches did not work well in bigger farms. Much of the river water did not get to the far ends of the farm. It soaked into the soil along the way. How could they keep the water from getting lost this way?

The Indians found a way of saving water. They put clay along the sides and bottom of the ditches. The clay kept much of the water from soaking into the soil. More water came to the plants. This was a good way. But people always like to make things better and better. You know that something happens to clay in water. It washes away a little at a time. It also lets some water soak through and get lost in the soil.

Baked clay is better. Baked clay does not wash away. The Indians built fires in the ditches to bake the clay.

In some parts of the country we can still use these ditches.

Irrigation Today

Ditches used for bringing water to plants are called irrigation ditches. Many farms today are watered by irrigation ditches. In many places there is good soil but very little rain. Irrigation ditches can make good farm land out of desert land. With more farm land, there is more food for everybody.

We build long irrigation ditches that bring water from many miles away. Even in the desert we can have farms that are miles away from a lake or a river.

In some places the water flows to the farms through big stone or concrete-lined ditches or through pipes. Then the farmer lets the water flow into smaller ditches between the rows of plants.

When the plants have had enough water the farmer stops the flow of water.

We can have good farms, even where the rivers dry up in hot weather. We can store the water in times of heavy rainfall and melting snow.

We store the water by building dams across rivers. The dams keep the water back. Storing the water also protects the land from floods. Without the dams, the rushing water fills up

the riverbeds and floods the land. Floods can wash away fields of grain and vegetables as well as roads and bridges. Floods can even wash away houses and leave people homeless. But when dams are built, the water is kept back and stored safely. The water then can be used when it is needed on farms and in cities.

In the building of dams and irrigation ditches, science has helped people.

Desert land has been turned into farm land by irrigation. Where cactus and scrubby bushes grew, there are fruit trees and vegetable gardens and fields of grain. The work of scientists has helped to grow food for more people.

Water for Drinking

Here is a lake behind a dam. The lake is full of cool, clean water. A few miles away there is a city where the people need the water for drinking. Should we use open irrigation ditches to bring the water from the lake to the city?

No, we should not! Dirt may fall in and make the water not fit for drinking. Drinking water must be very clean. We need something better than open ditches for bringing drinking water to the city.

We cannot use ditches for another reason. There are hills between the lake and the city.

Water Flows Down

Water cannot flow up over the hills in an open ditch. It can only flow down.

E X P E R I M E N T

You can see this for yourself if you crumple a piece of wax paper into the shape of a hill. Pour water over it.

You will see that the water always flows downhill. Water works its way down, never up.

All rivers and streams flow downhill. They do not flow uphill.

Making Water Flow Up

How can we get the cool, clean water from the lake to the city? We could dig a ditch through the hills, but that would be a lot of work and cost a lot of money. How can we get the water over the hill? Here is how you can find out.

EXPERIMENT

Join a rubber tube to a funnel.

Hold the tube in the shape of a hill. Be sure that the funnel is a little higher than the hill, as it is shown in the picture. Then pour some water into the funnel. Does the water flow out of the tube?

You will find that the water does flow out. When water flows through a tube or pipe, it can be made to flow up a hill as well as down.

Now we know how to bring the water from the lake to the city without digging through the hill. We build a pipe from the lake over the hill to the city. The water will keep flowing through the pipe, because the lake is higher than the city.

When the water gets to the city, it flows through pipes under the streets.

The pipes are called water mains. There are water mains under every street in the city. Each home and school, each store and factory, has pipes that reach down to the water mains.

Winter and summer, night and day, there is water for drinking and cooking and washing and playing. Water flows up into your bath-tub, up into the kitchen sink, up into the park fountain. Water goes up from the water mains under the street.

Water into the House

How can the water flow up from under the streets into the houses? Do we have to pump the water in some way, or can it flow up without being pumped? Here is a way to find out.

E X P E R I M E N T

Hold the tube as in the picture, with the open end over the pan. Pour water into the funnel.

You will see water flow out of the tube. Now lower the funnel. Does the water keep flowing?

When the water flows from a higher place, it presses against the water in the tube. It forces the water in the tube to flow up.

When water flows from a high lake, it presses against the water in the water mains. It forces the water in the mains to flow up into the houses.

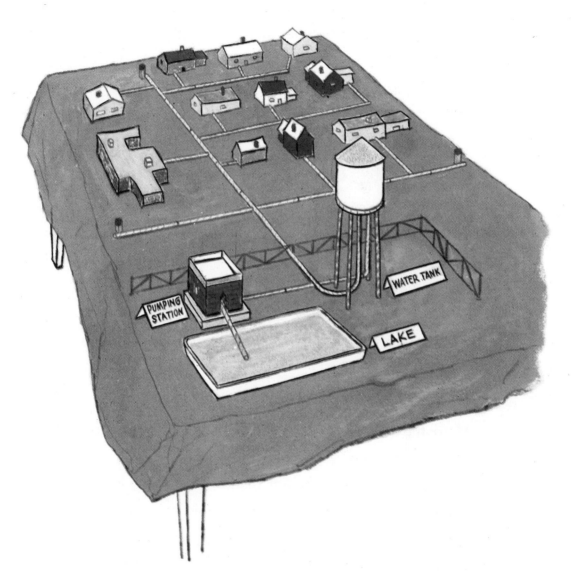

In some cities the water does not come from a high place. Then it cannot flow up by itself. We must force it up by a pump. Which way is used in your city, or in a city near you?

THINGS TO TALK ABOUT

1. Talk about the differences between rivers and lakes.

2. Talk about how you can help save water. At what time of year do we have the least water?

3. Irrigation is one way of watering plants. Talk about different ways of watering plants.

4. Talk about the different uses the farmer has for water.

5. Talk about the uses of a dam. Where are the Hoover Dam and the Grand Coulee Dam? Do you know of any other dams?

THINGS TO DO

1. Make a picture chart to show how water can be useful.

2. Count the number of times a day water is used in your home. What is the water used for?

Uses of Water in My Home	
1. Washing face, hands III	5. Watering plants I
2. Drinking IIII I	6.
3. Brushing teeth II	7.
4. Washing dishes III	8.

3. Dig a short ditch in the ground. Pour water into it. Notice how soon the water soaks into the ground. Put a layer of clay on the sides and bottom of the ditch. Pour water into it again. Notice how much longer it takes to soak into the ground. How did the Indians use this idea?

4. Make a book to show how water is used in the city and how it is used on a farm.

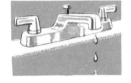

5. Do you have any places like this in your house? Measure the length of time it takes to fill a cup with water.

THINGS TO FIND OUT

1. Find out where the water goes after you let it out of the sink.

2. Find out how many different kinds of materials water pipes are made of. Why are some materials better than others?

3. Find out how your city gets its water. Where does it come from?

4. Find out where water is stored in your state. How is it stored?

5. Find out where the water in rivers comes from.

6. Find out where the water supply in your house can be shut off. Why is it good to know this?

SCIENCE AND CLOTHING

Look at us! All dressed up in our new clothes!

Look at us! All dressed up in our new clothes! What a difference!

People who lived long ago did not have very good clothing. The animal skins they wore did not fit well. They were not warm enough in cold weather. They were too hot for warm weather. And animal skins are very hard to get.

It was hard work for the father to hunt and skin enough animals to clothe his family.

Your father did not have to hunt and skin any animals to clothe you, because you are not dressed in animal skins. Most of your clothing is made of cloth.

Cloth did not just happen all of a sudden. People had to find out, bit by bit, how to make good cloth. They used science to help them find out how to make cloth and then how to make it better.

What Is Cloth?

Let's find out what cloth is made of, how it is made, and how science helped in making it.

You are wearing cloth. Look at it.

You can see that it comes in many colors. Some is shiny. Some is not.

Feel the cloth. Some is thick. Some is thin. Some is smooth. Some is rough. But all the cloth in your clothing is alike in one way. How? You can find out.

EXPERIMENT

Bring some small pieces of cloth to school. Pull them apart a little. You will see that they are all made of threads.

Pull some threads apart. You will see that they are made of separate threads twisted together. These separate threads are called fibers.

Where do fibers come from? They come from many places, even from you! Let's look at some fibers that you are making right now.

Hair Is a Fiber

Put your hand on your head. What do you feel?

You know, of course! You feel hair.

Hair is long fibers that you grew.

Hair has many colors. Some is straight. Some is curly. But it is all fibers.

Now look at the cloth. Cloth is made of threads, and threads are made of fibers.

We don't use our hair for cloth, but the Indians of the desert made cloth out of their own shining black hair. They cut it when it was long and made it into cloth. Cloth can be made out of hair!

People's hair does not grow long quickly. It would take you many years to grow enough hair to make a coat.

There are many other animals that grow much more hair than we do. Many people in many places found out how to use the hair of animals to make cloth. The Indians made cloth from the hair of dogs, goats, buffalo, and sheep. Here are some other animals whose hair is used to make cloth.

Mammals

Many animals grow hair. Such animals are called mammals. In the pictures you can see two kinds of mammals getting their hair cut. There are many other kinds of mammals, in many different shapes, sizes, and colors. But they are all alike in one way. They all grow hair.

Mammals are alike in other ways, too. Most mammal babies are born alive. Most other babies hatch out of eggs.

Mammal mothers can feed their babies with milk from their own bodies. No other animals can make milk.

Mammals' bodies are always warm inside, no matter what kind of weather it is outside. We say mammals are warm-blooded. Most other animal bodies are warm in warm weather and cold in cold weather. We say they are cold-blooded.

Thread from Insects

Some other animals make fibers, too. Here is a caterpillar beginning to make a house out of silk fiber that it makes itself.

The silk house is a cocoon. When the cocoon is finished you can't see the caterpillar.

In its cocoon the caterpillar will slowly change to a moth. Then it will come out of the cocoon and fly about.

The moth will lay eggs. Little caterpillars will hatch out of the eggs.

The caterpillars will eat and grow, eat and grow. Then they will make silk cocoons of their own.

Silk Moths and Silk

Many kinds of caterpillars make cocoons of silk. One kind makes silk that is very good for making soft, smooth cloth. This kind of caterpillar is called a silkworm.

People unwind the silk from the silkworm cocoons. They make the thread into silk cloth.

In many parts of the world the silk cloth is made into soft, fine clothing. The people of China found out how to raise silkworms and make silk more than three thousand years ago.

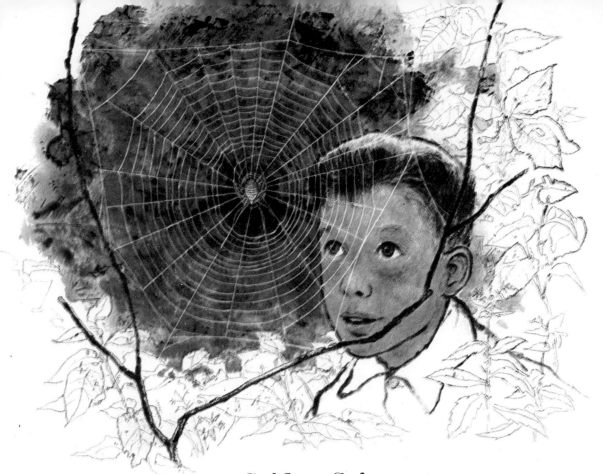

Spiders Spin

Here is another animal that makes silken fibers. You can tell that it is a spider by its shape and by its eight legs. A spider's fiber is a thin, strong silk. The spider spins it out of itself. It is like hair, but it is too much work to pick apart a web into its fibers. That is why we do not use it for making cloth. But spiders have many uses for it themselves.

Some spiders use their webs for catching food. One way is by building a sticky web to catch small insects.

Some spiders make a soft cocoon of spider silk to keep their eggs safe and dry. Baby spiders hatch out of the eggs. Soon each baby spider will send out long silken fibers. These fibers catch the wind and away sail the baby spiders. The baby spiders may sail a long way through the air. In fact, sailors have seen these fibers and spiders hundreds of miles from land.

Most spiders are very useful because they eat many of the insects that are harmful to plants or can carry germs.

Thread from Plants

We can make cloth out of plants, too. Plants do not grow hair, but they grow fibers of another kind. Here is how you can see bundles of these fibers.

EXPERIMENT

Get two fresh stalks of celery. Cut off the ends. Put one stalk into a glass with some red ink and leave it for a while. Look at the other stalk. You will see lines on it. Pull away some of these lines. If you could look very closely, you would see that the lines are thin tubes and fibers.

Why does a plant need tubes? Look at the stalk of celery in the red ink to find out. Cut through the stalk and look at the ends. You will find that the red ink goes all the way up the tubes to the very tip of the leaves.

Now you know what these tubes do. They help to bring things to the leaves. They are not there to bring ink, of course. They bring water and other things from the soil up into the leaves. Most of the plants that you know have these tubes.

EXPERIMENT

Here is how you can see more of these plant fibers. Get some stems and stalks from several different kinds of plants. Pull them apart the long way. You will find fibers in almost every plant.

You know how the tubes are useful to plants. The fibers between the tubes are useful to us. We can use them to make threads for making cloth. Indians pulled the strong fibers out of this desert plant to make string and cloth.

All over the world people have learned to use the fibers of plants to make cloth. This plant, called flax, makes a good strong cloth.

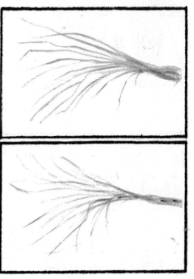

It is too much work to pull the threads one by one. Long ago people used science to make the work easier.

People found that soaking flax in water softened some parts of the plant. But it did not soften the fibers very much. Then the plants were dried in the sun. Next, the plants were pulled through a tool like a comb. The comb pulled apart each plant into its fibers.

The flax fibers were then twisted into longer, thicker threads that were made into cloth. The cloth was called linen. The linen was made into clothing.

Here is linen thread being made into linen cloth. Making thread into cloth is called weaving.

Cloth from Cotton

This is where your cotton socks come from. Of course you cannot see any socks yet, or even any cotton. But wait. When the cotton plant is ripe, the seed pods will pop open. On each seed there are many little white fibers of soft cotton growing. These fibers are light and fluffy.

The fluffy cotton is not quite ready to be worn on your feet. First it must be picked from the plant.

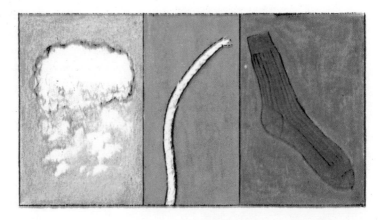

We Use Machines to Make Cloth

The seeds are combed out by a machine that looks like a round comb with many teeth. The short cotton fibers are combed out straight and then twisted together into long threads. Then, at last, the threads are ready to be made into socks for your feet or handkerchiefs for your nose.

EXPERIMENT

Take a piece of fluffy cotton. Pull away a little bit and begin twisting it into a thread. Keep pulling and twisting, to see how thin and smooth a thread you can spin. If you had time, you could learn to spin a really thin, smooth thread. But even then, think how long it would take to spin the thread for one of your dresses or one of your shirts.

Machines and More Machines

Today we do not have to spin threads or weave cloth by hand. We have machines that spin and weave much faster. We have other machines that can control the spinning and weaving machines.

These control machines almost seem to think. If a thread breaks, they stop the machine, tie a knot, and start the machine. They can do things that used to take many workers. They can put in spools and take them out. They can measure, pack, weigh, and load the cloth. One worker takes care of many machines that make cloth for many people.

New Threads from Many Things

We use science to find better ways of doing things. We have found better ways of making thread out of plant fibers and animals' hair. Now we have found ways of making thread out of many other kinds of things — out of bits of wood and straw, out of coal and sand, even out of milk or beans! It seems like magic, but it is not. When we find out how something happens, or how to make it happen, and why it happens, we are learning about science, not magic.

One kind of thread is made out of wood. The wood is boiled and mixed with other things until it is as soft as cooked cereal. Then it is squeezed out through tiny holes. It comes out in thin threads like food through a fine strainer. The thin threads are hardened. These threads are called rayon. Rayon is used for making many kinds of cloth.

Another kind of thread is made of milk! How can milk be made into cloth? You cannot easily turn a glass of milk into a handkerchief, but you can do one part of it. You can make a kind of thread out of milk.

EXPERIMENT

All you will need is milk, vinegar, and an eye dropper.

Fill the eye dropper with milk. Then hold the open end in the vinegar and empty it slowly. You will see the milk change. It becomes a thick thread. It's not much of a thread, and it comes apart when you pick it up, but at least it gives you a better idea of how threads can be made from milk.

You won't see any eye droppers in a factory where milk is made into thread. The milk is squeezed out of very, very small holes, into a liquid that makes the milk into very strong thread. Of course many other things are done to the thread before it is made into cloth.

We have used science to find ways of using sand, coal, and many other things of the earth for making cloth. Maybe you are wearing a coat that came from coal.

Now we can make thread from many different things. Some threads came from plants and some from animals and some from neither. We have used science to help us make these threads with less work for less money. Through science we find better ways of living.

THINGS TO TALK ABOUT

1. Talk about how the Indians got their clothes. How do we get ours today?

2. Talk about the ways people in different parts of the world dress.

3. Which of these are mammals? Tell how you know.

4. Tell about some insects and spiders that spin threads. How are the threads useful to them?

5. Birds are warm-blooded like mammals. In what ways do you think birds are different from mammals?

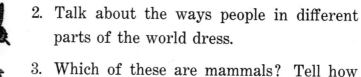

THINGS TO DO

1. Write down the kinds of clothing you are wearing. Then make a chart like this.

Clothing	What it is made of	Plant	Mammal	Insect	Man made
Shoe	leather		cow		
Sock	cotton	cotton			
Beads	plastic				plastic

2. Rub a piece of leather gently with a piece of sandpaper. Does it begin to look different? What does it look like?

3. Make a book. In it put little pieces of fur. Under each put or draw a picture of the animal from which it came.

4. Find a cocoon. Take it apart carefully. What is it made of? What is inside?

5. Man-made fibers are used to make many kinds of cloth. Make a collection of bits of this cloth and put them on a chart. Tell what they are made of.

THINGS TO FIND OUT

1. Find out what plants are used to make cloth and rope.

2. Find out how felt is made. Try this. Pull a piece of wool apart into separate fibers. Pat the fibers together until you have something that looks like felt.

3. Find out how weaving is done by hand. Try to weave a piece of cloth.

4. Find out what these words mean: tub-fast, vat dyed, sanforized, preshrunk.

5. Find out what a clothes moth can do to clothing. What kind of materials does it usually like? How can we protect our clothing from this insect?

THE OCEAN

Have you ever been to the seashore? Have you looked out over the ocean and wondered how big it is?

Have you tasted the ocean? When you get a mouthful of salty ocean water, you wonder, "How does it get so salty anyway?"

There are so many things to make you wonder — the waves, the sand, the strange shells and seaweed, the long-legged little birds that run right into the curl of the waves.

Let's wonder about the ocean.

How Big Is the Ocean?

Does the ocean have an end? We could find out by sailing a boat around the world. But you might not get home in time for dinner, so let's sail a paper boat around a globe.

Make a paper boat. Put it on the globe near land. Sail it away from the land. Look for the end of the ocean. Look for a place where you cannot sail around the land to another part of the ocean.

You cannot find such a place because all the oceans of the world are really one big ocean. Somewhere in each ocean there is a place where the water is joined to the water of another ocean. The ocean has no end.

Why Is the Ocean Salty?

Have you ever tasted ocean water? Then you know how salty it tastes.

Why is the ocean salty? Nobody knows all about it, not even scientists. But we do know that some of the salt came from the land.

How did the salt get from the land into the ocean? You know that most rivers flow into the ocean. As each river empties into the ocean, it carries a little salt with it. Where did this salt come from?

There is a little salt in some rocks and soils. Salt is a mineral. A mineral is a material of the earth that is neither plant nor animal. Rocks are made up of one or more kinds of minerals. Some minerals dissolve in water. Do you think salt dissolves in water? Try it.

The minerals become separated into such tiny pieces that you cannot see them.

When rain falls on rocks and soil, it picks up and carries away tiny bits of some minerals. We can get some idea of how this happens by doing an experiment.

EXPERIMENT

Cut off the tops of two milk cartons. With a large needle, put a few holes in the bottom of each. Put a handful of clean washed sand in each. Then mix a spoonful of salt with the sand in one of the cartons. Put both cartons on blocks of wood. Put a small cup under each carton.

Pour a half cupful of water into each carton. Let the water trickle through into the cups.

Take a tiny taste of the water in each cup. Is the taste the same?

The salt went into the water even though we cannot see it there. We say that the salt dissolved in the water. The sand did not dissolve.

119

Something like this happens when rain water flows through the soil. Of course, the soil is not so full of salt as the sand in your experiment was. There is only a very, very little, here and there.

As rain water flows over and through the soil, it picks up some salt and other dissolved minerals. It carries them to the rivers. The rivers flow on and on with their load of salt and other dissolved minerals. At last the rivers flow into the ocean.

The Ocean Has More Salt

Now we know that rivers carry salt and other mineral material into the ocean. The salt gives ocean water its salty taste.

But river water does not taste salty! Let's stop and think for a minute. River water usually has some salt dissolved in it, but river water does not taste salty. There is not enough salt in it to give it a taste. River water flows into the ocean, yet ocean water does taste salty.

Doesn't that seem strange? The water in the ocean came from rivers and rain, yet ocean water is very salty. Why is the ocean saltier than the rivers that feed it?

Let's find out how this can be.

EXPERIMENT

You will need a closed jar, an open bowl, a cup, and some salt.

Pour a cupful of water into the jar and another cupful into the open bowl. Dissolve one-half teaspoonful of salt in each of the containers. Taste the water in each container. Does it taste the same?

Close the jar and set it in a warm, sunny place. Set the open bowl next to it.

Leave both for two days or more. Then take out a spoonful of water from each. Taste each spoonful.

Do you find that the water in the open bowl tastes saltier?

Let's see what we can find out from this experiment. When the open bowl was left in a warm place, some of the water evaporated into the air. But the salt did not evaporate, at least not enough to make a big difference.

In the closed jar the water could not evaporate. The amounts of salt and water did not change.

Then you took out a spoonful of water from the jar and from the bowl. Did each spoonful have the same amount of salt in it? Which one had more salt in it? How did you tell?

Something like this happens in the ocean. The sun shining on the ocean makes the water evaporate. The salt does not evaporate. It stays in the ocean.

Day after day, year after year, the rivers of the world pour into the ocean. The river water has tiny bits of salt in it, not enough to taste. The water of the ocean keeps evaporating, but the salt stays. That is why the ocean is saltier than the rivers that flow into it.

Salt from the Sea

If you leave the salt water in the bowl long enough, all the water will evaporate. What will be left behind? Try it and see.

EXPERIMENT

The easiest way is to pour salt water into an open pan and let it stand in the sun. (If you are in a hurry you can boil the water.)

If you live near the ocean you can make real sea salt by evaporating the water out of ocean water.

Does this give you an idea? Could this be a way to get salt from the sea?

It could indeed, and people do it in many parts of the world. They let ocean water flow over flat beaches. They build low walls of sand or soil to keep the salt water from flowing back into the ocean. The water is evaporated by the heat of the sun, and the dry salt is left behind on the beach.

Where does the water go after it evaporates? You cannot see it because it evaporates in very tiny bits, too small to see, called water vapor. If you could see water vapor and follow it, you would travel to many strange and wonderful places.

The water vapor is carried up by air. Sometimes it forms into clouds up high. Sometimes it becomes fog that settles softly on roads and rivers. It may stay for a while or may drift across the sea to a land far away.

Sometimes big drops of water form in a cloud. Then rain will come pattering down on a ship at sea, or send a family hurrying back from a picnic. Perhaps the rain will make a farmer happy as it falls on a dry field of wheat. It may trickle into a mountain brook that flows into a river on its way to the sea.

Over and over again, the water keeps going on its never-ending travels. The water you washed your hands in this morning is millions of years old. It has been in many lands and many seas. Perhaps it was in a snowball thrown by a boy ten thousand years ago. Or it may have been in a puddle that you splashed in last week. Millions of times the water has traveled up to the clouds and down to the earth again.

Each of these millions of times, the sun warmed the water and sent it up into the air as clean water vapor. Each time, it turned again into clouds or fog. Each time, it was cooled and fell, clean and fresh, upon the earth.

Life in the Sea

When you go for a walk in the country, you can see many kinds of plants growing. You know that these plants are food for many kinds of animals. But when you stand at the seashore and look out at the sea, you cannot see any plants.

You may see a bit of seaweed drift by. In shallow places near the shore there may be some sea plants growing. That seems to be about all. Yet the sea is full of plants. Some that grow near the shore are quite large, but most of the plants that grow in the sea are so small that you cannot see them.

There are millions of plants in a glass of sea water. They are tiny green plants that look like this, but they are much smaller.

You cannot see these tiny plants, but all the animals of the sea depend on them. Tiny water animals eat the tiny plants. Bigger animals eat animals that eat these tiny plants. And these bigger animals are food of still other animals.

If there were no plants growing in the sea, there could be no fish, no shelled animals, no sea life of any kind.

The tiny green plants of the sea float in the water. They take in minerals from the water. They also take in a part of the air that dissolves in water. The sun shines on the green plants and helps them to grow.

The tiny green plants become food for the tiny animals. These tiny animals in turn are food of other animals. No matter what food a sea animal eats, it depends on plants.

If there were no plants, no sea animals could live. But there are many, many plants — millions in a glassful of sea water. There is food for many, many animals in the sea.

Many Animals from the Sea

If you ever visit a fish market, you can see a few of the many, many different kinds of animals that come from the sea.

There are fish in many colors and shapes and sizes. And there are the shelled animals, such as oysters, which look like ragged rocks, and scallops shaped like pretty little fans. Perhaps you have been a little frightened by a lobster waving a huge claw, or a crab that suddenly clicked its blue legs.

In some markets you can see even stranger sea animals. Squids and octopuses, shrimps and snails, clams and mussels — all these are only a few of the sea animals that are sold as food.

People have been getting their living from the sea for many, many years. But you cannot just pick fish as you pick berries. You must know the ways of the fish you are trying to catch.

People in many countries live near the seacoast and eat sea food. They have found out many things and have shared what they learned with other people.

Life of the Salmon

Long ago these people of the seacoast learned the ways of the salmon. They knew that grown salmon live in the ocean, far from the shore. They come up the streams only when they are ready to lay their eggs. The Indians learned what time of year the big salmon came. Then they were ready and waiting with their nets and spears.

In the quiet water of brooks and pools the
salmon lay their eggs.

When the baby salmon hatch out of the eggs
they live in the brooks and fresh-water streams,
eating and growing.

Then they swim out
into the ocean.

When they are fully grown, they journey
back to fresh water to lay their eggs.

Mammals of the Sea

The biggest animal on land or sea is the whale. Whales have to come to the top of the water to breathe. They have to do this because they are not fish, but mammals.

A fish can get air from the water. But a mammal must come up to the top to breathe. A mammal cannot get air in water. Perhaps you found that out when you tried to swim underwater. You could stay under a little while, but then you had to come up to fill your lungs with fresh air. Your lungs can hold enough air for you to stay under water about half a minute.

Whales can take huge breaths into their lungs, and can stay under water for fifteen minutes or more. But they must come up at last. Then they let out their breaths. What a huge breath! Like your breath, it is full of bits of water. On a cold morning your breath makes a little cloud when you breathe out. The huge breath of a whale makes a big cloud. This cloud is called a spout.

The Indian hunters, watching for a whale to come to the top, could see the telltale spout, and would go after the whale. When the hunt was over, the whale was pulled to shore. Then there was a huge feast of whale meat for everybody. After that they all went to work, cutting up huge pieces of whale fat, and cooking it down to oil. The oil was a good food that did not spoil quickly.

Most of the whale's fat is in a thick layer just under its skin. You know that whales are mammals, not fish. Mammals are warm-blooded. Their bodies always have to be warm even in cold water. Fish are cold-blooded. Their bodies are as cold or as warm as the water that they swim in.

Like all other mammals, whales breathe air, and they are warm-blooded. Whales are mammals in other ways, too. Their babies are born alive, not hatched from eggs. The babies are fed with milk from the mother's body. And whales have hair! Oh, very little, just a tiny one here and there. But each one is a hair, and only mammals have hair.

Many other mammals besides whales live in the sea. Here are some of these mammals.

Manatee

Dolphin

Porpoise

Sea Otter

Seal

THINGS TO TALK ABOUT

1. Talk about how the ocean is different from a lake. How is it different from a river?

2. Tell why people like to swim in the ocean. What safety rules must you keep in mind when you go swimming in the ocean?

3. Talk about people who make a living by working on ships or where the ships are loaded. What kind of work do they do? How do these people help us?

4. Talk about other mammals besides whales that live in the sea. How are sea mammals different from fish?

5. Talk about the travels of the salmon. Do other sea animals travel? Why do they travel so far?

6. This animal does not eat plants. Yet if there were no plants in the sea, it could not live. Tell why this is so.

THINGS TO DO

1. Salt is sometimes put on icy sidewalks. To find out why, put two pieces of ice in a dish. Sprinkle salt on one piece. Which piece of ice melts sooner?

2. Put a small glass of fresh water and a small glass of salt water into the freezer. Which one freezes first?

3. Make a chart to show all the things we get from sea animals and plants.

4. Make some tests to find out what things can dissolve in water. Some things will dissolve easily, some will not dissolve easily, and some will not dissolve at all. You may try flour, soap flakes, oil, sugar, salt, and paper. Try other things, too. Make a chart of what you find out.

THINGS TO FIND OUT

1. Find out why waves are bigger and higher at some times than at others. Why do the waves often have white tops or "caps"?

2. Do this experiment to find out why ships must watch out for huge blocks of ice. What are these blocks of ice called? Put a piece of ice in a glass of water. Does it float on top of the water or is most of it under the water?

3. Find out the uses of seaweeds.

4. Find out what birds live near the ocean. What do they eat?

LEARNING ABOUT LIMESTONE

Sea Shells

You can find sea shells in many different shapes, colors, and sizes. But they all are alike in two ways. All are the homes of sea animals. All are made of a hard, stony material. This same material is found in a stone called limestone.

Sea animals make their hard shells out of lime dissolved in sea water. You cannot see or feel this dissolved material, yet a sea animal builds a stony shell out of it.

How is this possible? You can find out by doing an experiment with lime.

EXPERIMENT

Get some limewater. This is lime dissolved in water. You can buy limewater at the drugstore. It is quite cheap and cannot hurt you even if you drink it. A half glass will be enough for your experiment.

Look at the limewater. You will see that it is clear, like drinking water.

Put a drinking straw into the limewater and blow. Something in your breath changes the limewater. The material that makes this change is called carbon dioxide.

Keep blowing until the limewater stops getting milkier. Then stop blowing. Let the limewater stand for a while. Soon you will see tiny white grains sink to the bottom.

Pour off the water, and let the tiny grains dry. Limestone is made of tiny grains like these.

You blew your breath into the limewater and got tiny grains like those in limestone and sea shells.

The carbon dioxide from your breath came together with the lime in the water and made stone — limestone.

Sea Animals Build Shells

Sea animals have almost the same things that you used in your experiment. They build their stonelike houses in almost the same wonderful way. All around them is sea water with lime dissolved in it. The animals have carbon dioxide in them. This is the same material that you blew out in your breath. The carbon dioxide and the lime come together inside the animals and form their shells. Bit by bit, as the animal grows bigger, its shell house grows bigger, too.

You Make Limestone

Sea animals are wonderful! But you are just as wonderful. You, too, build something that is hard and stonelike. You, too, as you grow bigger, make this something bigger. This stony something is not a shell outside of you. It is the bones and teeth inside of you. Your bones and teeth are made of minerals that are almost the same as limestone. Right now, this very minute, your body is making these materials and building bones and teeth with them.

You know that sea animals use lime for making their shells. And you know that they get it from the sea around them. But you do not live in the sea. How do you build bones and teeth?

Our bones and teeth contain a mineral called calcium. Lime, limestone, and sea shells also contain calcium.

How We Build Bones and Teeth

You get calcium from the food you eat and drink. Many kinds of plant and animal foods have calcium in them. The food that has the most calcium is milk. That is why milk is so good for people whose bones and teeth are still growing.

There is calcium in milk and milk comes from cows. How do cows get calcium? They get it in the grass and other plants that they eat. The plants get it from the soil. The calcium in the soil dissolves and soaks into the roots. Then it passes through the tubes into the rest of the plant. When we eat the plant, or when we drink the milk from the cow that ate the plant, we get the calcium that we use for building our bones and teeth.

Minerals Go Out of the Soil

Plants get calcium and other minerals from the soil. Every time a plant is pulled up by a farmer, minerals are taken away. Every time a cow bites off a blade of grass, minerals are taken away. After a while, will all the minerals be gone and the soil become useless? Can such a thing happen?

Yes, it can and does happen. If a farmer keeps taking away plants from the soil and does not put anything back, the soil becomes poor. It does not have enough minerals for the plants growing in it. The farm land becomes useless for growing plants.

We Put Minerals Back into the Soil

But good farmers do not let the soil become useless. They put minerals back into the soil. The farmers do this by spreading minerals over the soil. Rain water dissolves the minerals and carries them down into the soil. Then the soil has minerals for growing plants.

Where do we get the minerals to put back into the soil? There are many kinds of minerals that come from many places. Let's see where we get one mineral, calcium.

Calcium for the Soil

Here is a mountain of limestone. Limestone contains large amounts of calcium. Machines dig the limestone out in huge pieces and other machines crush it and heat it. It becomes a white powder that dissolves easily when it is spread on the soil. This is one of the ways we get calcium for the soil.

How were the mountains of limestone made? They were made under the sea, partly from the shells and bones of sea animals. This land, where now there is a mountain, was once covered with water. Many sea animals lived here, and layer upon layer of their bones and shells became pressed together.

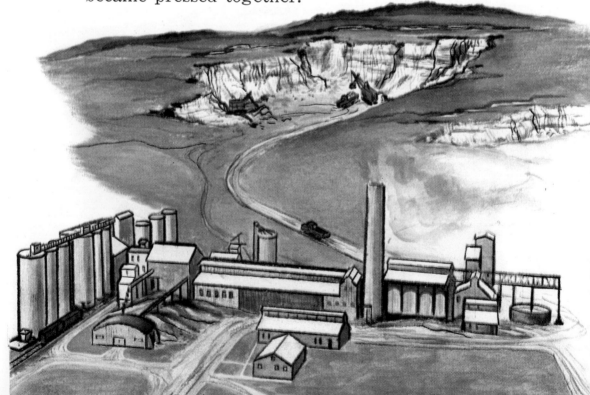

Later, the land rose above the sea. The layers containing the bones and shells became mountains of limestone.

Calcium Journey

What a long trip the calcium has taken! From the sea water it went into the shells and bones of sea animals. The shells and bones piled up in the sea. Slowly these piles became mountains of limestone. Now, is the trip over, or does something else happen to the calcium?

The calcium keeps going. Even if people did not cut limestone out of the mountains to get calcium, it would not last forever. You know that mountains are slowly being worn away.

Heat and cold break the stone a little at a time. The roots of plants grow into the limestone and make it crumble. The wind blows sand against it and scratches off little pieces.

Water can even dissolve limestone in the way that it dissolves salt. This happens very, very slowly, but it has been happening for millions of years. It is happening right now.

Huge limestone mountains are slowly being broken into bits and dissolved.

What happens to the dissolved limestone? Some of it soaks into the soil with rain water. Plants get their calcium from this dissolved limestone in the soil.

Some of the dissolved limestone trickles with the rain water into brooks that flow into the rivers. The rivers flow into the sea.

There it is, back where it started from. You know that the mountains of limestone were made of bones and shells of sea animals that lived millions of years ago. These animals used the calcium from the limestone dissolved in sea water when they made their bones and shells.

Now the calcium is back in the sea water again, millions of years later.

There are other sea animals that will use the calcium for making their bones and shells. What do you think will happen next?

Over and over again, the things of the world are used, and changed as they are used, and used again and again. Nothing is lost.

THINGS TO TALK ABOUT

1. Talk about foods that are made from milk.

2. Tell how shells are useful to water animals. Why must the shells be hard and strong?

3. Talk about the ways you can keep your teeth strong and healthy.

4. Tell about shells you have found. Where did you find them?

5. Tell the story of the calcium that is in a bottle of milk.

THINGS TO DO

1. Make a book of pictures to show animals that have bones and animals that have no bones.

2. Put some water plants into a large jar of pond water. Get some snails and keep them in the jar for several weeks. Look at the snails every day. After a while, baby snails may be born. You can watch the baby snails grow bigger every day.

3. How is the shell of a hen's egg liks a sea shell? Do this experiment to find out. Put a piece of egg shell into a small jar of vinegar. In another jar of vinegar, put a piece of sea shell. Does the same thing

happen in both jars? What do you think the egg shell is made of? Why?

4. Make a chart of pictures of food rich in calcium.

5. You can test stones to see if they are limestone. Squeeze a slice of lemon or pour vinegar over the stone. If it bubbles, your stone has limestone in it.

THINGS TO FIND OUT

1. Find out how caves are formed in limestone mountains.

2. Find out how many teeth you have in your mouth. How many teeth should you have when you are grown up?

3. Find out how these animals get the calcium they need.

4. Find out what sort of rock was used in building your school. Was any part of it built with limestone or marble?

5. Find out what coral is and what it has to do with limestone.

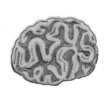

6. Find out how lime is used in building a house.

7. Find out how the farmer puts calcium into the soil. What does he use?

KEEPING FOOD

Too much to eat, then not enough to eat.
That was how people lived a long, long time
ago. When the Indians killed a large animal,
there was too much to eat. The people ate and
ate, but could not finish all the meat. They had
to leave the rest to spoil.

When fruits and berries became ripe, the same thing happened. Again there was too much to eat. Some could be eaten, but the rest was left to spoil.

If only food could be kept from spoiling! Then there would not be times of too much to eat, and times of too little.

How could food be kept from spoiling? The Indians found out some ways, and so did other people. They tried one way and another, and told each other what they found out. Little by little we have found out what makes food spoil and how we can keep it from spoiling. You can find out, too.

What Makes Food Spoil?

EXPERIMENT

Let's spoil some bread to see what happens. Moisten a slice of bread and put it in a dish. Let it stay in the open air for an hour. Then cover it and put it in a warm, dark place for a few days. Do you see something fuzzy on the bread?

This is bread mold. The bread mold does not taste good and it is not good for you to eat. The bread mold has spoiled the bread for eating. Let's look at the bread mold with an instrument that scientists use. It is called a magnifying glass, because it makes things look larger.

We can see that the bread mold is a plant. It has many little branches and roots. The round, dark things are full of tiny dots called spores.

Spores are something like seeds. When the spores are ripe they fall out. If a wind catches them, they are carried away until they fall somewhere. These spores are too tiny to see, but the air is full of them.

If spores from bread mold fall on bread or some food like bread, they begin to grow. Then the food has been spoiled by mold.

Can you tell why we keep food covered?

Mold plants are not the only plants that can cause food to spoil. You can see mold easily, but the other plants that spoil food are too tiny to see even with a magnifying glass. If we can keep all these little plants from growing on food, we can keep the food from spoiling. We know some things that are not good for most kinds of plants. Perhaps these things are not good for mold plants, either. Let's see.

EXPERIMENT

We know of many plants that cannot live without water. What will happen to the spores of mold plants with no water? Get two slices of bread. Toast both slices a little to make them very dry. Moisten one slice and put it in a dish. Put the other slice in another dish but do not moisten it.

Leave both slices in the open air for an hour or two. This will give time for many spores to fall on both slices. Then put a cover over each one and put both away in a warm, dark place for a few days.

On which slice did mold grow?

Drying Food

Indians dried many foods in the hot sun. Now can you tell why?

You have eaten many kinds of dried food, too. Here are some foods before and after drying. They can keep because mold plants cannot grow without water.

Smoking Food

Perhaps on a cloudy day long ago a busy mother thought of hanging fish over a fire to hurry the drying. Or perhaps someone looking at the trees around a campfire saw that the leaves were dry but not burned. Who knows how? But in some way people found out that smoking and drying together make food taste better and keep better. Smoked and dried meats and fish gave people food that lasted through the winter.

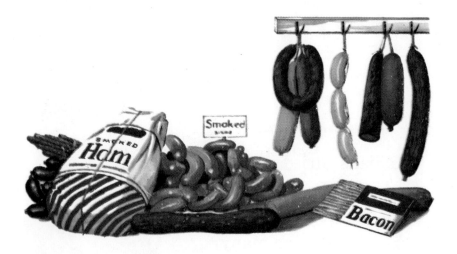

Smoking and drying help keep food good to eat. Molds and the other little plants that make food spoil cannot grow well on dry, smoked food. Smoked food does not spoil easily.

Indians also used salt to keep some foods from spoiling. Where do you think they got the salt? Why did salt keep food from spoiling? We can find out if salt will keep some plants from growing.

EXPERIMENT

Take two bean plants. Water one with salt water and one with fresh water. What happens?

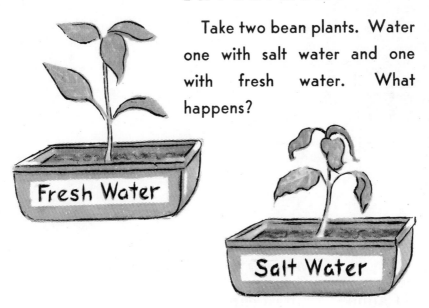

Most plants do not grow well in salt. People salt fish and many other foods to keep the plants that spoil food from growing on the food. Salted foods do not easily spoil.

Cooking and Canning

Canned fruits, canned vegetables, canned soups, canned meats — how many kinds of canned food have you eaten?

Canning is a very good way to keep food from spoiling. In fact, canning does two very good things. In canning, the food is first cooked for a while. This kills the tiny plants that would make the food spoil. Then the food is packed in cans or jars so that other tiny plants in the air cannot get in.

Keeping Food Cold

Keep food cold enough, and it won't spoil. People found that out a long time ago. They kept the food as cool as they could in cellars. They also cut ice out of frozen lakes and packed it away in sawdust. In summer they used the ice in iceboxes to keep food cold.

Today we have many more ways of keeping food cold and fresh. Kitchen refrigerators keep food from spoiling for a short while.

Freezers, which are much colder, freeze the food and keep it good for many months.

Many foods are shipped in refrigerator cars, refrigerator trucks, and even in refrigerator ships. All kinds of delicious fresh and frozen foods are shipped from one part of the country to another without spoiling. The food doesn't spoil because mold and the other tiny plants that cause food to spoil cannot grow in the cold.

That is why we can have almost any kind of fresh food at any time of the year.

Smoking, drying, freezing, canning, and salting! These are some of the ways people have found to keep food from spoiling.

Because people watched, and tried, and thought, and shared what they learned, we all eat better all through the year.

THINGS TO TALK ABOUT

1. Talk about the differences between a refrigerator and a deep freezer.

2. Tell how science has made it possible for us to eat many kinds of foods all the year.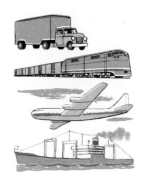

3. Talk about the ways in which food is shipped from different parts of the country.

THINGS TO DO

1. Here is the old-time way of drying apples. Cut an apple into thin slices. Run a needle and thread through the pieces. Hang them up to dry in the sun for a week. Why do the pieces get thinner? Feel them.

2. Use a thermometer to find out how cold it is in different parts of your refrigerator. Where is the best place to keep ice cream, meat, milk, celery?

3. Try this. Get the kind of bag ice cream is taken home in, a plain paper bag, and a saucer. Put ice in each. Note the time it takes the ice to melt completely in each.

4. Put a tablespoonful of fresh chopped meat in one jar. In another jar put a tablespoonful of fresh chopped meat that has been mixed with a tablespoonful of salt. Leave for a week. What happens?

5. Make a book of pictures which show ways of keeping food fresh and good to eat.

THINGS TO FIND OUT

1. Find out ways the Indians kept food good to eat. How were their ways like ours? How were they different?

2. Find out what food was served on sailing ships a hundred years ago. What food is served on ocean liners today? Why?

3. Find out some ways of keeping fish good to eat.

4. What has to be done to vegetables to get them ready for freezing in a home freezer?

5. Find out the different kinds of materials in which food is wrapped and kept. How do these keep the food fresh and clean?

LAKE AND STREAM

Do you live near a place like this? Have you ever visited such a place? It is so quiet! It seems as if you are alone. But there are many animals that live here. Under the water there is a busy world of living things. There are plants and animals that have ways of living in the water.

Fish

No matter where an animal lives, it must have some air. Animals get oxygen from the air. Oxygen is the part of the air that animals need in order to live. Fish live in water, and they must have air from which they can get oxygen. Is there air in the water? Here is how you can find out.

EXPERIMENT

Fill a drinking glass with water and let it stand for a while. Look at it. You will see bubbles along the side of the glass. These are bubbles of air that came out of the water.

You cannot take oxygen from the air that is in water, but a fish can. A fish has special parts, called gills. Water passes over the gills, and the oxygen in the water goes into the gills. In this way fish can get oxygen from the water. They do not have to come up for air.

Even when the water is covered with ice, fish can get oxygen. There is enough air in the water for the fish because in winter they do not move around much. When fish lie quietly  they need very little air. When you lie quietly, do you breathe slowly or quickly?

EXPERIMENT

Jump up and down or run around. Do you breathe slowly or quickly? Do you use more oxygen when you lie quietly or when you jump up and down or run around?

You have heard people say, "He is a very good swimmer. He swims like a fish." But only another fish can really swim like a fish.

Fish are built just right for swimming. They have strong tails, which help them speed easily through the water.

Fish have fins, which help to keep them steady and stop them quickly.

You can find out how a fish uses its fins for stopping.

EXPERIMENT

Get two large sheets of cardboard and hold them down against your sides. Start running fast.

While you are running, spread out your arms and hold the cardboards straight out, as the boy in the picture is doing. You can feel how the cardboards push against the air and make you slow down.

When a fish needs to stop suddenly, it spreads out its fins. The fins push against the water and slow the fish down, just as the cardboards slowed you down.

The fish moves through the water easily. The fish's scales are smooth and they overlap. There is very little rubbing between the fish and the water.

Many fish have a long rounded shape and a pointed head. These fish can swim very fast.

Can you tell which of these two fish is shaped for faster swimming?

Can you tell which of these boats is shaped for speed?

Can you tell why an airplane is shaped like this?

Frogs

Now you see it, now you don't! You can easily see a frog when it jumps or swims, but not when it sits quietly on a green lily pad. A green frog on a green plant can sit and catch insects with its long tongue. A bird flying overhead, looking for a frog lunch, cannot easily see it.

But look at the underside of the frog. It is almost white. Is this a help to the frog? Here is how you can find out.

EXPERIMENT

Get a sheet of white paper and a sheet of dark paper. Take them outside and hold them over your head. Which one is harder to see against the bright sky? You will find that it is harder to see the white paper.

In the same way, it is harder to see the white underside of a frog. A fish looking for a frog to eat cannot see it easily because the fish is underneath, looking up at the frog, against the bright sky.

White underneath and green on top are good frog colors for living in the water. Some other water animals, too, are dark above and light below. This helps them to live safely in water.

Insects

Buzz! Buzz! Slap! Slap! Why are there so many insects around a lake? Wherever you see many insects you can be sure that there is plenty of food for them. Insects that eat plants can find many plants in the lake and around the lake. Insects that eat other insects can find plenty of food. There is food around the lake for insects.

There are many, many places for insects to lay their eggs. Some lay eggs right on the water.

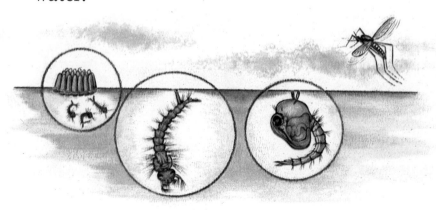

Some insects lay eggs along the leaves and stems of plants that grow in the water and around the lake.

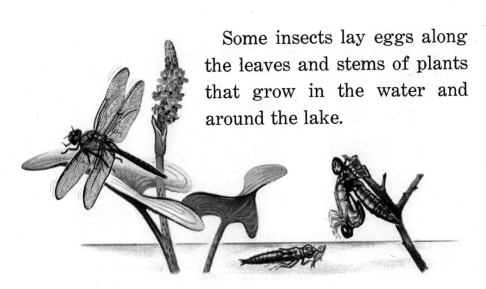

When the eggs hatch, there is plenty of food for the growing insects. That is why there are many insects around a lake.

There are many, many kinds of insects. There are more insects than any other kind of animals. They come in many sizes and shapes and colors. Some swim, some fly, some crawl, some jump, but all insects are alike in three ways.

Insects are born from eggs.

Insects have six legs when they are grown.

Insects have three parts to their bodies.

A Little Lake

Have you ever wished you could see what goes on down in a pond? You can have your wish if you make a pond of your own in a glass tank. Such an indoor pond is called an aquarium.

You can buy everything you need to fill your aquarium from a pet shop. Or, if you can get some help, you may be able to find plants and animals in a pond.

If you go to a pet shop, find out which fish do well together. Find out which water plants are best. In the picture there are fish which some children bought in a pet shop.

To make an aquarium you will need a very clean glass tank.

Put about two inches of clean, washed sand into the aquarium.

Get some water plants from a pond or a pet shop. Set the plants into the sand. Clean, smooth little pebbles will hold the plants down.

Now set the aquarium where it can get light. All green plants need light.

Now you are ready to put in the water. Get water from a clear stream or pond if you can. If you use tap water, let it stand in an open jar or pan for a day.

Put a sheet of paper over the plants and pour the water in slowly. You can put your water animals in after the plants begin to grow and the water is clear.

Here are some pond animals that can live in an aquarium. Find out what each one eats. If you put in a turtle, it should be a very small one. Big turtles eat little fish. The turtle will need a rock or a piece of wood, because turtles have to come up for air. They have no gills, so they cannot get oxygen from the air in water. Feed the turtle bits of meat, vegetables, and ripe fruit every day or two. This will keep the turtle from nibbling the fish.

After your aquarium is all set up, you will enjoy looking at it. You will be able to see what goes on under the water without having to be under water yourself. Here are some things you can find out about your water plants and animals.

Fish in the Aquarium

Look at a fish. Look at its shape. See how it pushes itself by waving its tail. How does it use its fins for stopping? See the smooth, shiny scales. Tell why they help.

Watch the fish as it moves its mouth. It is not drinking the water that it takes in. Each mouthful of water flows over the gills and then out through the opened gill covers. What does the fish get from the water?

Can you tell if the fish likes to hide in the shade of the plants? Does the fish nibble at the plants?

Tell what you can about the eyes of the fish.

Snails in the Aquarium

Watch the snails crawling along. They have feelers that help them find out about the things ahead of them. They have eyes that can tell light and dark.

When the snail is floating, tap it. Watch how it sinks. It lets out a bubble of air and takes in a drop of water. This makes the snail heavier and it sinks.

Touch the tip of a feeler with a pencil, gently. How does the snail protect itself?

You may see little patches on the glass that look like tiny bits of jelly. These are snail eggs. Watch them for a few days. Do you see tiny spots on them? With a magnifying glass you can see that these tiny spots are baby snails inside the eggs.

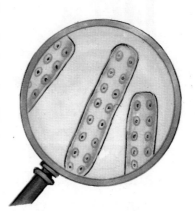

Watch the snail eating a leaf. You will find that it eats the soft parts but not the tubes. These are too hard for the snail.

The snails are useful workers in an aquarium. They help keep the water clear. They crawl up and down the sides of the tank, eating tiny plants that grow there. Too many of these plants would make the water cloudy and green.

Sometimes you will see snails crawling over the sand, eating the tiny plants that may be growing in the sand.

The snails are the clean-up workers of the aquarium. How do you think they are useful in a pond or lake?

Water Plants

You know that land plants have roots, stems, and leaves. Most water plants do, too! You can see the ways they have for living in water.

Look at the stems. Can you see that the stems of the water plants bend easily? Do you think this is a help to them when the water flows back and forth?

The leaves of most water plants are not held up by stiff, hard stems. The leaves are held up by the water.

Look at the leaves of a water plant. They stay bright and green in the water. Do you think a land plant would stay green underwater? Try it with a little land plant in a jar of water.

You know that a land plant gets water through its roots. Its roots get water from deep in the soil. The roots of some land plants grow very deep. Do you know what kind of roots a water plant has? Pull up one of the plants to see. You will find that some of the water plants have only little roots. Some water plants have no roots at all. Water plants get most of the water they need through every part of them.

The more you look at them, the more you will find that water plants are built right for living in water.

Water Birds

Quack, quack, and dig, dig. The ducks are busy with breakfast. With their bills the ducks can scoop up mouthfuls of mud from the lake bottom. In each mouthful there are bits of plants, and perhaps an insect or two.

A duck's bill is like a strainer. It lets the mud strain out into the water, but it keeps the food. Scoop and strain, scoop and strain, a duck's bill works well for a duck.

Some birds have bills like soup ladles which they use for scooping up small fish.

This bird's bill has sharp ridges like teeth which it uses for holding small fish.

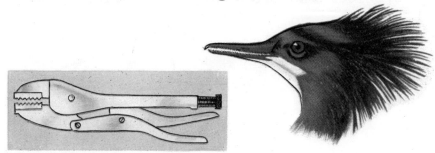

This bird is a great fisher, too. It has a strong beak that helps it catch fish.

This bird lives near water, but it doesn't feed on fish. It has a beak that helps it get insects and the seeds of weeds and wild rice.

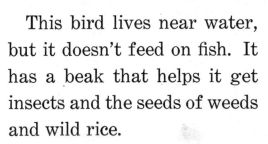

Many birds that live near water or on water have special feet, called webfeet.

Webfeet are fine for swimming along in the water.

Webfeet also are a help in walking on soft mud.

These sharp claws can catch a fish and hold it tight.

With its long legs, this bird can walk in shallow water.

Water birds have oily feathers, and they have ways of keeping their feathers oiled. You can find out how oil helps a water bird.

EXPERIMENT

Get two small pieces of newspaper. Rub oil on one piece. Then sprinkle water over both pieces. Which paper soaks in the water?

What would happen to a water bird's feathers if they were not oily?

Water birds have water ways.

Mammals of Lake and Stream

Here is a beaver being busy as a beaver. It is busy cutting down trees with its sharp teeth. It is making a safe, dry home out in the water. Animals that hunt beavers cannot easily get into the beaver's home because the door is underwater.

With its webfeet and wide tail, the beaver is a good swimmer. It also uses its tail for something else. When it slaps its tail on the water, the little beavers hear the sound and hurry home.

Here are some other mammals that often live near water. They all like fish. And each has its own way of catching them. In what ways are these mammals alike?

THINGS TO TALK ABOUT

1. Talk about what happens to the animals in a pond in winter.

2. Talk about animals and plants you have seen in or near a lake.

3. Talk about ways we control insects that harm us.

4. Tell how these animals help us.

THINGS TO DO

1. In the spring you can find frogs' eggs. Keep them in a large jar or aquarium full of pond water. How are these eggs different from those of a hen? Watch to see what hatches. Do they look like frogs?

2. Make up meal cards for a robin, frog, bear, beaver, and sunfish. The card should tell what each animal likes to eat. See if your class can tell by the card which animal it is for.

3. Make a book of bird pictures to show how the feet and bills of birds help them to get the food they need.

4. Visit your neighborhood fish store to see the different kinds of fish sold there. How are the fish different? How are they alike? Find out where they came from.

5. Make a collection of insects in your neighborhood. Tell what each of these insects eats.

6. Watch an aquarium. Try to see if you can find the answers to these questions. How does a fish move? How does it stop? Does a fish have ears? Can a fish close its eyes? What does a snail eat? How is it useful? How does it move?

7. Make a book called, "Lakeland and Pondville Who's Who." In it put pictures of birds, insects, and other animals that live in or near a lake or pond.

THINGS TO FIND OUT

1. Find out which birds can swim. What helps them to do this?

2. Find out how beavers can help prevent floods.

3. Find out on which part of an insect's body its wings are found.

4. Find out which plants live completely in the water, have only their roots in the water, or live on top of the water.

5. Find out which insects can dive, swim under the water, or walk on top of the water.

YOUR TREES

This city family is all ready for a vacation in the woods. With the things they brought from the city, they can have a good vacation. But what would happen if they had no city things?

Long ago, Indians lived here. They knew how to get what they needed from the forests and lakes. They caught animals for food and clothing. They learned how to use trees for building homes, for making boats, and even for food. They shared what they learned, and they lived well.

Lake and Forest Indians

The forest Indians knew how to use trees. They knew how to use the bark of the tree for many things. If you look at the trees that grow near your home and school, you can see that there are many kinds. Each kind of tree has a different kind of bark. Bark is a sort of skin that protects the inner parts of the tree.

Bark protects the inside of the tree from insects and other animals that like to eat it. It also protects the tree just as wax paper protects a soft sandwich. It keeps the inner part of the tree from drying out.

Indians who lived where birch trees grew used large strips of birch bark to cover their houses. Can you tell why? They taught the settlers how to make bark houses like the one in the picture on this page.

The Indians also used birch bark for their canoes. Birch bark is smooth and thin; it pulls off in large strips that can be made into a boat shape. And it is waterproof, which is a nice thing for a boat to be.

Why Boats Float

Will the canoe float or sink? When an Indian built a canoe, he knew that it would float. Every part of the canoe was made of bark and wood, and the Indian knew that wood floats.

But he would have been surprised if he could have seen a boat made of metal. Metal does not float. How can a boat made of metal float? Let's find out.

EXPERIMENT

You will need a piece of metal foil about half as big as this page. This kind of metal foil comes in rolls and is used for covering food. You will also need a few coins, or nails, or other small pieces of metal.

Fold the piece of metal foil into a flat-bottomed boat, as in the picture. Put it in a pan of water. Does it float? Now put a few coins or other bits of metal into the boat. Does it still float?

Your flat-bottomed boat floats well because it is spread out. It is spread out on top of a large amount of water. It pushes aside a large amount of water. The boat does not weigh more than this large amount of water, and so it can stay up. It does not sink.

Now take out the metal boat with its little load of metal. Fold it over and over into a small bundle with its load of metal inside. This bundle weighs the same as before, but it is smaller. Put it in the water. Does it float?

When the boat is small, it is not as spread out as before. It pushes aside only a small amount of water. The boat and its load are heavier than this small amount of water. So the boat sinks.

Metal or wood, big or little, a thing floats when it does not weigh more than the water it pushes aside. If it weighs more, it sinks.

Looking inside a Tree

Every tree has many parts. You know the bark protects the inside of the tree. The leaves make the food that the tree uses. To do this, the leaves must have sunlight. They need water and minerals, too.

The water and minerals come into the tree through the roots. But the water and minerals and the roots are in the ground far away from the leaves. In a tall tree they are very far away. How do the water and minerals get all the way from the roots up to the leaves? You can't climb inside a tree to find out, but you can find out with a small part of a tree.

EXPERIMENT

You will need two freshly cut twigs with leaves on them. You will also need two glass jars, water, and some red ink.

Put one twig in a jar with some red ink, and the other in a jar with some water. Let them stand overnight.

Do you find new red or dark brown lines in the leaves of one of the twigs? These lines show where red ink flowed into the leaves. How did the ink get all the way up? Find out by cutting the twig down the middle. Do you see that part of the twig is red all the way from bottom to top?

In the red lines of the leaves and twigs are tiny tubes — tiny end to end tubes. Trees have millions of tubes. Water and minerals from the soil travel from the roots to the leaves in these tubes.

When new leaves are formed, new tubes are made in the twig, too, and all the way to the roots. The new tubes are made just inside the bark. Along with the tubes wood fibers grow also. The wood fibers make the tree strong.

Every year a new layer of tubes and fibers grows around the tubes and fibers of the year before. That is why a cut tree looks like this. Each layer is one year's growth of tubes and fibers.

These layers are the wood of a tree. The wood of a tree is made mostly of tubes and fibers. You know how these are useful to the tree. Do you know how they are useful to you?

There are thousands of tree tubes and fibers in your wooden pencil, and millions of them in your wooden table. Even the paper of this book is made of these tubes and fibers. You can see them by tearing a bit of newspaper. Hold it in front of a light and look at the torn edge. This is how the torn edge looks under a strong magnifying glass.

Can you see the fibers and tubes that once were wood?

How can a piece of hard wood be made into a sheet of white, soft paper? First the wood is ground into very small pieces. Next the pieces are cooked and beaten until the tubes and fibers come apart from each other. Then the tubes and fibers are put together into sheets of paper.

Would you like to make a few sheets of paper? It's not very hard to do. You can't begin by breaking a big log apart into its millions of tubes and fibers, of course. You would need big machines to do this. So let's use the wood tubes and fibers that we can find in paper handkerchiefs.

EXPERIMENT

You will need: an empty milk carton, a piece of nylon stocking, a stapler, a mixing bowl, an egg beater, two blotters, a round glass jar, and some paper handkerchiefs.

1. Cut the bottom out of the carton, like this.

2. Cut the sides away, to look like this. This will be the holder.

3. Cut another piece that fits into the bottom. Cut out most of the piece, so that it looks like a picture frame.

4. Stretch a piece of nylon stocking over this frame and staple it.

5. Put the frame into the holder.

Now you're ready for the raw materials. Since we can't begin with logs as they do in a paper factory, we will use paper handkerchiefs. Tear two and a half handkerchiefs into small bits and put them into a quart of water. Beat it with the egg beater until it is all smooth, without lumps or bumps. Now you're ready to turn it into paper.

1. Dip the holder and frame into the bowl.

2. Hold the holder straight up and lift it out slowly. Let the water drip out.

3. Gently lift out the frame from the holder.

4. Put a blotter on the frame. Then turn it over.
5. Roll it with the round jar.
6. Gently pick up the frame. Your newly made paper should stay behind, on the blotter.
7. Put another blotter on the new paper.
8. Put a heavy book on this sandwich. Leave it for a day until it is dry. Or you can speed up the drying by asking a grownup to press it with a warm electric iron.
9. Pick up the top blotter. Then lift the new paper from the lower blotter. You have made your own paper!

Perhaps you will want to make some more paper, just for fun. For your second try, add a bit of water color before using the egg beater. This will give you colored paper. Also add a few spoonfuls of liquid starch, to make the paper more smooth. Do you want some shiny paper? Then add a spoonful of gelatin powder.

Hard and Soft Wood

Different kinds of trees make different kinds of wood. If you have worked with wood you know that some kinds are harder to cut than others. You may wish to find out about the hardness of wood.

EXPERIMENT

Bring in some pieces of different kinds of wood. Get some thumbtacks. Press a tack into each piece. How can you tell that some kinds of wood are harder than others?

When scientists want to find out about the hardness of wood, they do not use thumbtacks. They use a special hardness-testing machine. You can make one almost like it.

KIND OF WOOD	NUMBER OF HITS
PINE	
OAK	
SPRUCE	
MAPLE	
HICKORY	
ASH	

EXPERIMENT

You will need a hammer, a piece of string, and a small steel ball, like the ones in a skate wheel.

Put the steel ball on the piece of wood you are testing. Hold the hammer like this and let it drop. When the hammer hits the ball, it will drive the ball a little way into the wood. Lift the hammer again, just as high as before, and let it drop again. Keep on doing this until the ball is driven all the way into the wood. How many blows of the hammer were needed? Now test other kinds of wood. Does a softer piece need more blows or fewer?

Sugar from Trees

Long ago the Indians made maple syrup and maple sugar from the sap of maple trees. They showed the early settlers of this country how to make them, too. Today, farmers still make syrup and sugar from the sap of the maple tree.

Early in the spring, the trees are full of sap. Sap is a watery liquid with a little sugar in it. The sugar will be food for the young leaves that will open out when warm weather comes. Sugar-maple trees make so much sap that we can take some of it and still leave enough for the young leaves to use.

To get the sap, a hole is drilled in the trunk of the tree. The sap drips out, a drop at a time, into buckets. How can the sugar dissolved in the sap be taken out?

Heat Changes Many Things

Heat can make the change. Maple sap is heated to make the water evaporate. If we evaporate part of the water we will have maple syrup left. If almost every drop of water is evaporated, we get delicious light-brown maple sugar. You can make maple sugar yourself by slowly heating maple syrup, stirring it slowly as the water evaporates.

Heat can change other things besides maple syrup. In your kitchen, heat changes foods in many ways.

How does heat change the color of some foods?

What are some foods that become softer with heating?

Can you name a food that becomes harder when it is heated?

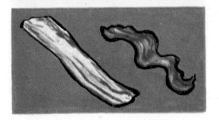

How does heat change the taste of some foods?

THINGS TO TALK ABOUT

1. Talk about how we use the forests today for things we need. How did the Indians use the forests?

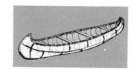

2. Tell how a walk in the forest is different from a walk in the city. What are the things you can see, smell, hear, and touch in each?

3. Tell why a forest is a good place for some animals to live.

4. Talk about things you have seen changed by heat.

THINGS TO DO

1. Make a collection of pictures of things made of wood. Then make a chart showing which of these things are made of soft wood and which are made of hard wood.

2. Look for places where tree roots have lifted sidewalks.

3. Make a chart of the things in your classroom that come from trees.

4. Collect different kinds of tree seeds. Plant some to see if they will grow.

5. Make leaf calling cards. Put different kinds of leaves on cards. Put their names on the backs of the cards. See if you can tell what leaf it is by its shape.

6. Make a book which shows different kinds of paper. Tell what each is used for. Of what is the paper made?

THINGS TO FIND OUT

1. Find out why pine trees in a forest grow so tall and straight.

2. Find out how many different kinds of animals use trees for homes. Look for these homes. How many can you find near where you live?

3. Find out what these words mean: deciduous, evergreen. These words tell about certain trees. How many different kinds of these trees grow in your neighborhood?

4. Find out all you can about this plant. Does it always have the same color, size, and shape? Does it always grow on the ground?

KEEPING WARM IN WINTER

Catching a furry animal is not easy. Making it into a fur coat is lots of work. Why did Indians go to all that trouble? And why do people today? You know why. Fur can keep you warm in cold weather. But why is fur so warm? You can find out.

First look at a piece of fur. You can see that it is really two things. It is a piece of leather and it is also a thick mat of fluffy hairs.

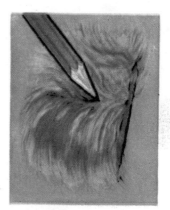

Let's see how fluffy hairs help to keep us warm.

EXPERIMENT

How do the fluffy hairs help? You can find out with two pieces of thin cotton cloth and two jars of the same size.

Wrap one piece of cloth as tightly as you can four times around one jar.

Wrap the other piece of cloth loosely four times around the other jar.

Fill the jars with hot water.

Put the cover or lid of each jar on tightly. Leave both jars for half an hour.

Now take off the jar covers. In which jar is the water warmer? Use a thermometer to find out.

Did you find that the water in the loosely wrapped jar stays warm longer? This is because there is more air trapped between the cloth and the jar.

Air does not let heat pass through easily.

Is there air in fur or wool to keep the heat from getting out? You can find out.

EXPERIMENT

For this experiment you will need a small piece of fur. If you have no fur, wool will do. Both wool and fur are mammal hairs and both are fluffy.

With a pencil, push the fur or wool down to the bottom of a glass of water. Hold it there. Do you see a lot of bubbles coming up?

These are bubbles of air. Wool and fur, and other fluffy materials, have lots of air trapped among the hairs. When you wear woolen or fur clothes, you are also wearing lots of trapped air.

Trapped Air for Warmth

The trapped air helps to keep the heat in you. Your body makes heat. You are a mammal and all mammals make heat. Furry or woolen clothes keep the heat of your body from getting out, and so you feel warm.

E X P E R I M E N T

Push a small piece of cotton cloth into a glass of water. Do you notice that there are not so many bubbles as there were in the wool experiment? There is little air trapped in the cotton threads. That is why cotton is not so warm as wool or fur.

Now you know one reason why wool has more warmth than cotton. Do you know why fur has more warmth than cotton?

Trapped Air Everywhere

You have seen how trapped air holds the heat of your body. It also works for you in many other ways.

Pot holders are made of fluffy cloth with plenty of trapped air to keep the heat of the pot from passing through into your fingers.

Many houses are built with fluffy material in the walls and under the roof. This helps to keep the heat of the house from getting out in winter. And it helps to keep the heat of the sun from getting into the house in the summer. Look around you to see how many things have trapped air in them.

You know that wood is made of millions of tiny tubes, side by side. Once the tubes had sap inside; now they have air. With millions of tubes full of trapped air, wood should be a good material for keeping heat from passing through. Let's see if this is so.

EXPERIMENT

You will need a short wooden pencil, a nail about as long as the pencil, and a cup of hot water.

Hold the pencil and nail part way in the water for a while. Does the wooden pencil become warm? Does the nail become warm?

The wood has air in the tubes. The nail has no tubes and no air. Again we see that trapped air keeps heat from passing through. Now can you tell why the handles on steam radiators are often made of wood?

Fire

All ready to light! The small dry bits of bark will catch fire easily, and the big pieces of wood will burn a long time. But bark and wood will not catch fire by themselves. Heat is needed to start a fire.

You can start a fire with the heat of a burning match. But before there were matches people had other ways. The boy in the picture is making a fire in the way that many Indians used.

Back and forth, back and forth, the string spins the stick. The spinning point rubs against the block of wood.

Rub your hands together. Feel how warm they get. The point of the stick becomes hot from rubbing against the wood.

In the hole in the wood there are bits of dry grass or other things that catch fire very easily. With something to burn, and heat to start it, we can get a fire going.

What is happening here? There are things to burn, and plenty of heat. But when sand is put on the fire, the fire goes out. Why does the sand make the fire go out? You can find out by doing an experiment.

EXPERIMENT

Here, too, there was something
to burn and plenty of heat. But
the fire went out. The glass jar
shut off the air. In the air there is
oxygen. Without oxygen a fire
goes out. When sand was poured
over the campfire, the oxygen was
shut off and the fire went out.

We need three things for a fire. We need
something to burn. This is called a fuel. We
need heat to start the fuel burning, and we need
oxygen from the air.

Can you answer these questions about each
of the fires in the pictures?

What fuel is being burned?

How does air get to the fire?

Do we use the fire to give us heat or light?

How is the fire started?

Heating Buildings

It's fun to sit in front of a campfire and warm yourself. Nobody sits in front of this fire, and yet it warms many people in many rooms of a school building.

This fire is burning in a furnace. The furnace is in the cellar of a school building.

What fuel is being burned? Is it the same as that burned in your school? Are there special ways for letting in air?

The heat from the fire will warm the classrooms all through the building. How can the heat travel so far? Here is how you can find out.

EXPERIMENT

Heat some water in a teakettle. Hold an empty glass bottle near the spout of the kettle. Does the bottle soon become hot? What came into the bottle to make it hot? Where did the steam come from?

When water is heated very hot, it turns to steam. The steam pushes its way up and makes other things hot. It made the bottle so hot that you soon had to put it down.

In the same way, fire in a furnace heats water and turns it to steam. The steam pushes its way through pipes that go up to the classrooms.

The pipes are joined to radiators. The steam from the pipes flows into the radiators and makes them hot. That is how a fire in the cellar can send heat to rooms up above. The heat is carried by the steam. Does steam carry the heat in your school?

A radiator is at one side of the room. How does the rest of the room become warm? You can find out with two blackboard erasers.

EXPERIMENT

Hold the blackboard erasers over a hot radiator or an electric light. Clap the erasers together to make the chalk dust fly.

You will see the chalk dust move with the air. Do you see the chalk dust moving up over the hot radiator or lamp?

This is because the air is moving up. When air is heated, it moves up. It rises.

If you could follow the moving air, you would see it flow up higher in the room and then move across to other parts of the room. The warm air warms the things along the way.

Now hold the erasers under the warm radiator or lamp. Clap them again.

Do you see chalk dust moving toward the warm radiator or lamp? The chalk dust is being carried by cool air moving in.

Near a warm radiator, there is cool air moving in and being warmed when it touches the warm radiator. Then it moves up and out into the room.

Over and over again, the air keeps going in a circle around the room, giving its heat to the things in the room and then coming back to the radiator again. In this way the radiator can heat the whole room.

Fire Safety

A fuel, oxygen, and heat — bring these three together and you have a fire. Take away any one, and the fire is out.

All the rules about safety with fires are rules about fuel, oxygen, and heat. Here are some fire-safety rules. Can you tell how each rule helps?

1. Pour sand over a campfire when you are through using it.

2. Do not keep paper, or other things that can burn easily, near a furnace.

3. If a person's clothes are on fire, wrap him in a blanket or rug.

4. If you see or smell smoke coming through a closed door or window, do not open it.

5. Do not play with matches.

Find out about more fire-safety rules in your school and town. How does each rule help?

THINGS TO TALK ABOUT

1. Talk about all the different ways fires can be started.

2. Tell why children must not play with matches. How should matches be stored?

3. Sometimes your bed may be cold when you get into it. Tell how the bed gets warm after you have been in it for a few minutes.

4. Tell why a fire in a fireplace is not the best way to keep a house warm. Why is a fire in a furnace better?

5. Tell how you could use each of these to put out a fire: a rug, sand, water, a blanket, salt.

6. Talk about different kinds of fuels that can be used for making fires.

THINGS TO DO

1. Look at the handles of pots, pans, cooking tools, and radiators in your home. What materials are these handles made of? Why?

2. Many boy scouts know how to start a fire with a spinning stick. Ask a boy scout to come to your class and to show how this is done.

3. Make a picture map to show how your house is heated. Show where these things are: radiators, the furnace, the thermostat, the pipe that leads to all the radiators from the furnace, and the place where the fuel is stored. Put in anything else you think will help to show how your house is heated.

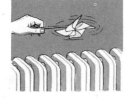

4. Make a pinwheel of paper. Hold it over a hot radiator. What makes it move?

5. Do the experiment on page 220 but also use an empty tin can. Count how long you can hold the bottle before it gets too hot to hold. Do the same with the tin can. Does this experiment help you to understand why radiators are made of metal?

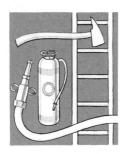

THINGS TO FIND OUT

1. Go on a trip to a firehouse. Find out several ways that firemen use to put out fires. What tools do they use?

2. Find out why steam pipes are often covered with a white material. What kind of material is it?

3. Find out what fuel is used to heat your house. Where is this fuel stored?

4. Find out how storm windows and doors help to keep a house warm in winter.

MACHINES

Levers

Hurry, hurry, hurry! See the great Strong Man, the Muscle Man! See what the Muscle Man can do with his muscles!

See him lift a full-grown man.

See him tear apart a piece of hard steel.

See him go faster than the fastest runner in the world.

See him do other amazing things as well.

227

Where can you see this wonderful, amazing person?

Just look in the mirror. You are the Muscle Man! You can lift a full-grown man.

This is how you do it.

EXPERIMENT

Put a long board on a block of wood. Ask the man to stand on one end of the board. You push down on the other end. Watch the man rise. You lifted the man with your own muscles.

Of course, you used a board and a block of wood to help you. But these things did not make your muscles stronger. They helped you to use your muscles as if they were stronger. Let's see how.

EXPERIMENT

Put the board on the block of wood in this way.

The block is close to the middle of the board. Try to lift the man. Do you find it hard to do?

Now put the block back close to the other end, as you had it in the first experiment. Notice that you are far from the block, but the man is near it.

Which is the easier way to lift the man?

A block and board used in this way is called a lever. When the block is far from you and near to the man, the lever helps you to lift him. The lever is helping you to use your muscles as if they were stronger.

Here is a big stone to be pushed out of the way. It is too heavy to lift without the help of a lever. But we have an iron rod and a smaller stone. How can we use them to make a lever?

Shall we place them like this?

Or will this way work better?

In which way does the lever help us to use our muscles as if they were stronger?

Not all levers are long. Here is a short tool being used as a lever to pry off the lid of a can. The lid is not heavy, but it is stuck on too tightly to pry off easily.

Not all levers are straight. Here is a lever with curved parts for pulling out nails. Nails are not heavy, but you cannot pull them out of wood with your fingers. You need a lever to help you use your muscles as if they were stronger.

Sometimes we use two levers together. These pliers are two levers. In fact, this tool is called a pair of pliers. Pliers are not for lifting or prying. Yet they do help you to use your muscles as if they were stronger.

Sometimes we use levers to help us in another way. We use them to move something more quickly than we could with our muscles alone. Let's see how a lever can do this.

EXPERIMENT

Hold a long stick near one end, as in the picture.

Keep one hand still, and with the other hand move the stick up and down a little way, slowly. Look at the far end of the stick. You can see that when your hand moves a little way, the far end of the stick moves a greater way. The far end is also moving faster than your hand.

This boy is using a lever to help him move something quickly.

The lever is a fishing rod, and the something is the hook at the end of his line. He wants to pull the hook up fast, before the fish has time to get away. A small move of the boy's hand makes a big quick move of the far end of the rod, the fishing line, and the hook.

So you see, levers can be useful in two ways. They help us to move something more quickly, or they help us to use our muscles as if they were stronger. Both ways make work easier for us.

Wheels

You know that wheels are useful in many ways. Just to remind yourself, look at this picture. Find all the things that move with wheels. How would the moving of things be different if there were no wheels?

Faster With Gears

Beat, beat, beat. This is a slow way of mixing a cake.

Here is a faster way, and wheels make it faster. Let's see how the wheels help.

Notice the teeth on the big wheel of a beater. See how they fit into the teeth on the little wheels. These wheels with teeth are gears.

See how the handle turns the big gear. What do the teeth of the big gear push? When the smaller gears turn, what else turns?

Now let's see how this kind of beater saves us work when we want to mix something.

EXPERIMENT

Make a mark on one of the blades of the mixer. Turn the handle slowly.

Count the turns of the blade. How many times does the blade turn while the handle turns just once?

When the big wheel turns once, the little wheel turns many times. Each turn of the handle makes many turns of the blades.

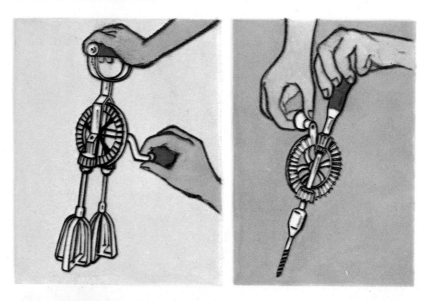

A hand drill, too, has a big and a little gear.

When a big gear turns a little gear, the work is speeded up.

Good-by to three wheels! Now he's big enough for four wheels.

Can you find the four wheels on the new bicycle? There are two big wheels that roll along on the ground. There are also two smaller wheels that do something else. Let's see what they do.

Look at wheel 1 and wheel 2. Notice that both wheels are gears. A chain goes around both gears. The chain fits the teeth of both gears.

When gear 1 is turned, it moves the chain. What does the moving chain do to gear 2?

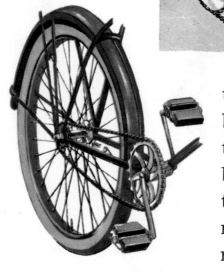

Gear 2 is really part of the big back wheel of the bicycle. When gear 2 turns, it makes the whole back wheel turn, too. As the back wheel turns, it makes the whole bicycle move.

Now you understand how your feet turn the wheels of your bicycle. But what do you gain by riding on a bicycle instead of walking? Let's find out.

EXPERIMENT

See how far you can go when you take two long steps on foot. Then take two steps on a bicycle. You do this by starting with one foot at the top. Push your foot all the way down and then all the way up.

How far did you go in two steps on the bicycle? How far did you go in two steps on foot? What helps you go farther and faster on a bicycle than on foot?

Wedges

Here's a fine dry log for the fire, but it is much too thick to catch fire easily. It has to be split into thinner pieces. The strongest man you can think of is not strong enough to tear it apart with his bare hands. He needs something that will help him to use his muscles as if they were stronger.

Here it is. It is an ax. The head of an ax is thin and sharp along one edge. It gets thicker and thicker toward the other edge. This shape is called a wedge.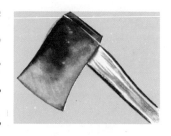

When you use a wedge, your muscles are strong enough to split hard wood. With a wedge you can even split rock and steel! Let's look more closely at the wedge.

A wedge really does two things, one after the other. First the thin sharp edge makes a thin cut in the wood. Then the thicker part of the wedge spreads the wood apart. Cut and spread, cut and spread. Wedges help you to use your muscles as if they were stronger.

The wedge is such a useful tool that people make it in many sizes and shapes, for cutting many kinds of materials. What are these wedges used for?

Here is a tool that has hundreds of little wedges in a straight line.

Each little wedge splits off a tiny piece of wood. When you use a saw, you can see a stream of these tiny pieces falling. What are they called?

Some wedges are made with a sharp point instead of a sharp edge. Can you tell how these pointed wedges are used?

Some wedges are grown by plants and animals!

Can you tell how each of these wedges is useful to the plant or animal?

THINGS TO TALK ABOUT

1. Tell why you must be careful in using some wedges. What safety rules must you follow when you use these wedges?

2. Tell how the Indians moved things. Did they use wheels?

3. Tell what machine you would use to
   a) open a tight bottle cap
   b) crack a nut
   c) break a rock
   d) lift paint to the top of a building
   e) whip cream

4. Talk about your toys that have wheels. Bring some of your toys to school and tell the class how they work.

THINGS TO DO

1. Ask your father to show you all the tools in his toolbox. Can you tell which are levers and which are wedges? Find out what the tools are used for.

2. Get a screw, a screwdriver, and a piece of wood. Use the screwdriver to turn the screw. Which way must you turn the screw to make it go into the wood? Which way must you turn the screw to take it out of the wood? Do all screws work this way? Find out.

3. Try to cut a piece of cardboard by using the tips of some scissors. Now try to cut the piece of cardboard by using the part of the scissors near the screw. Which is easier? Why?

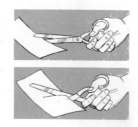

THINGS TO FIND OUT

1. Look at the experiment on page 236. Plan the same kind of experiment with a bicycle. How many times does the back wheel turn when your foot goes around once? Is it the same for every bicycle?

2. Find out what things in your house have wheels.

3. Find out about the different kinds of nails used by carpenters and builders. Get one of each kind and make a chart. Tell how each is used.

4. Find out how these levers work: crowbar, monkey wrench, and nail puller.

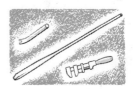

5. Find out where it is best to sit on a seesaw. Have a friend sit near the middle. Push at the other end and try to lift him up. Now have your friend sit at the end of the seesaw. Push down again on the other end. Which time was it easier?

SOUND

It is early morning and everything is still. It seems as if there is not a sound in the world. But there is! Do you think the cat hears? What does the dog hear? What would you hear in such a place on a quiet morning?

There are many different sounds in this quiet little place. Maybe the robin hears an earthworm digging a tunnel in the ground. Perhaps the cat hears a tiny click, click sound as the robin hops along the path. The dog can hear the soft swishing sound of the cat's paws as it slinks through the grass.

We do not often hear such soft sounds as these in our noisy world. Mostly we hear loud sounds. Bang, clang! Splash, crash! Ring, sing! Clatter and patter!

Sounds are so different and they are made by so many different things in so many different ways. And yet, here is a strange thing. All sounds are alike in one way. How are they all alike? Let's try to find out.

How Are Sounds Alike?

EXPERIMENT

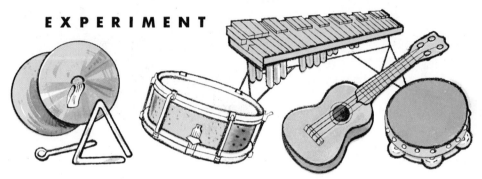

You will need some of these sound-makers. You will also need a piece of thread and some grains of cereal.

Put a few grains of cereal on the middle of the drum. Then strike the drum near the edge. What happens to the cereal? What made it move like that?

A drum makes a sound when the drumhead moves quickly up and down. You cannot easily see the drumhead moving, but you can see that it makes the cereal move.

Now hold your hand flat on the drumhead and do the experiment again. Your hand keeps the drumhead from moving as much as it did before. Does the cereal jump as high? Is the sound as loud?

Do the other sound-makers also make sound by moving quickly? This is how you can find out. Tie a thread to a grain of cereal. Hold it like this, near a sound-maker. Then strike the sound-maker and see what happens.

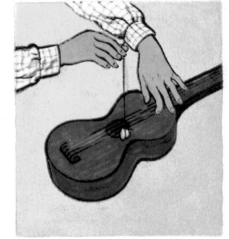

This is how to hold the cereal with a string sound-maker.

Each of these sound-makers makes sound in the same way. Something moves very quickly back and forth, or up and down. We say that it vibrates. To make sound, something has to vibrate.

Hold your fingers like this and buzz like a bee. Can you feel the vibration from your own sound-maker?

How Does Sound Travel?

What a loud roar a jet airplane makes as it speeds through the air! That roar is made by vibration like any other sound. The spinning jet engine makes vibrations. These vibrations make the loud roar that booms in your ears.

But the airplane is high up, far away from you. How does the sound travel from the airplane to you? Through what do the vibrations travel? Here is how you can find out.

EXPERIMENT

You will need a sheet of paper, a watch, and a handkerchief.

Roll the paper into a tube. Hold the watch at one end. Put your ear to the other end. Do you hear the watch ticking?

What is inside the paper tube? Nothing but air. Do sound vibrations travel through air?

Now roll the handkerchief into a tight round roll. Open the paper tube and put the handkerchief in the middle. Roll the paper into a tube again. Now can you hear the ticking of the watch? How far did the sound vibrations from the watch travel before they were stopped?

Does Sound Travel Through Water?

This skin-diver can tell you whether sound travels through water. But he is a little busy right now; so let's find out in another way. Next time you take a bath take a coin or a pebble with you. Sit up in the bathtub and tap the side with the coin or pebble. You can hear the tapping, of course. Now duck your head until your ears are covered. Tap the bathtub again. Can you hear the tapping? Your ears are covered with water, so the sound could not have come through the air. How did it come? How loud is the sound? Does the sound travel better through water or through air?

Can Sound Travel Through Other Materials?

These two space travelers are making important plans. They are planning their first trip to the moon. They know that there is no air on the moon. They know, and you know, that sound travels through air. How will they talk to each other when they get to the moon?

Will our space travelers just have to wave their arms in a helpless way? Or is there some other way of talking to each other? Does sound travel through other things as well as air? Let's help the travelers. Let's find a way for them to talk on the moon.

EXPERIMENT

You will need a plastic ruler, a wooden ruler, a piece of cotton, a piece of sponge rubber, a handkerchief, a large nail, and a pencil. You will also need someone to help you.

Put your head down, with one ear pressed against the table. Cover your other ear. Let your helper tap one end of the wooden ruler. The other end is pressed against the table. Does sound travel through the wooden ruler and through the table?

Now lift your head and listen to the sound. It is coming to you through the air. Which way is louder? Does sound travel better through air or wood?

Now try the plastic ruler. Does sound travel through hard plastic?

Now try it with the cotton, like this.

Try the sponge rubber in the same way. Then try the handkerchief, folded into a ball. Try other soft and hard things. Does sound seem to travel better through soft materials or hard materials?

Could the space travelers talk to each other in this way?

How does this help you to catch a little more sleep?

This Indian is listening for footsteps. Why does he put his ear to the ground?

Talking Through a String

You have found that sound can travel through wood, hard plastic, and other materials. Sound can sometimes travel through thread and string, too. You can make a toy telephone that works with a piece of string.

EXPERIMENT

You will need two paper cups, two toothpicks, and a piece of thin string about six feet long. Push a hole in the bottom of each cup, using a toothpick. Pass an end of the thread through each hole. Tie a toothpick to each end of the thread.

Now you and your helper hold the two cups as in the picture. The string must be tight.

Take turns talking to each other and listening. Does sound travel through a string that is pulled tight? Does it travel through a loose string? Does it travel through the tight string when somebody touches the string? Can you tell why?

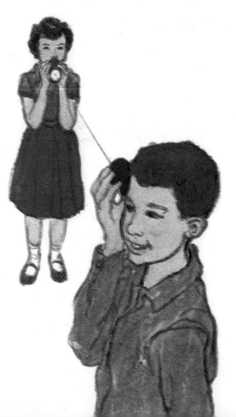

Would you like to make a four-way telephone? Here it is. Be sure that all the strings are pulled tight.

String telephones cost very little. Shall we use them everywhere? Before we decide, let's think about these things:

What will happen to the sound vibrations when a flock of birds perch on the wires?

How would you stretch a straight string to your friend who lives around the corner?

In your experiment you used a six-foot string. Try a much longer one. Does the longer string carry vibrations as well as the short string?

Real telephones are different. Real telephones are not joined to each other by strings. They are joined by wires that carry electricity. Before you say hello there is a steady flow of electricity. When you speak into a telephone, your sound vibrations make little bursts in the steady flow of the electricity. There is one burst for each vibration. You cannot hear these bursts of electricity as they zip swiftly through the wires.

The bursts of electricity from your telephone reach the other telephone very quickly. They cause a part inside the other telephone to vibrate. This makes the air vibrate. Then the other person hears what you are saying.

Telephone wires can go around corners without losing their electricity. The electricity is not stopped or changed when the wires hang loose or touch something. The wires can be laid over high mountains or deep underground, or even at the bottom of the ocean. You and your friend can talk to each other from halfway around the world!

Does Sound Take Time to Travel?

When somebody talks to you, do you hear the sound right away? Or do you hear it a tiny bit later? Here is an experiment that will help you to find out.

EXPERIMENT

You will need a drum or a large metal pail, and something to strike it with. You will also need someone to help you.

Go to a large open place, such as a park. Stand near your helper while he strikes the drum or pail. You seem to hear the sound right away. Now go far away from each other and try again. Do you hear the sound right away, or does it take a little time to reach you? How can you tell? What happens when you go still farther away?

All Kinds of Ears

Your ears look very nice on you. The rabbit's ears look just as nice on the rabbit. How would it be the other way? Would you hear differently if you had a rabbit's ears? Let's make a paper rabbit ear and find out.

EXPERIMENT

Make a paper horn like this. Stand at one end of the room. Put the horn against one ear and cover the other ear with your hand. At the other end of the room somebody is to make a soft sound. This can be the tapping of two pencils, or the ticking of an alarm clock. The person then comes closer and closer to you. How close is he when you first hear the sound?

Now do the same experiment without the paper horn. Do you find that the sound-maker must be closer to you before you hear the sound? How does your big paper ear help you? How do a rabbit's big ears help it?

How are their large ears helpful to these animals?

Helps to Hearing

Some parts of your body make very soft sounds as they work. Your heart goes lub-dup, lub-dup, lub-dup. Your lungs make a low windy sound. Your doctor listens to these sounds through a stethoscope. Let's see how a stethoscope is useful to him.

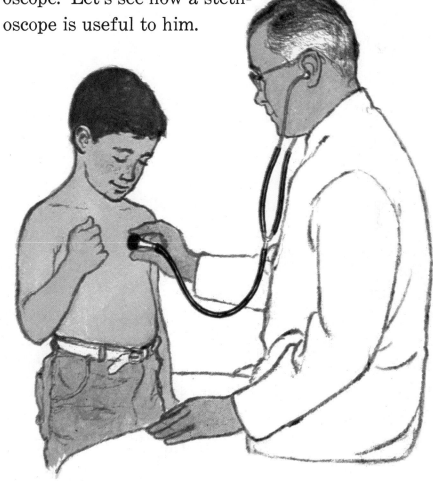

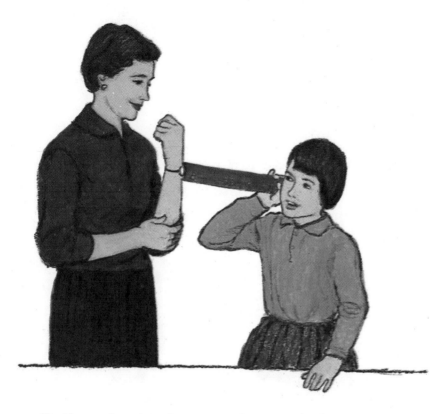

Roll a sheet of paper into a tube. Put the tube over a watch. How well do you hear the ticking of the watch? Now listen to it without the tube as far away from it as you were before. Can you hear the ticking just as well?

Without the tube, the sound of the ticking spreads out on all sides. Only a small part of the sound reaches your ears. With the tube, the sound does not spread out. More of it reaches your ears. How does the doctor's stethoscope help him to hear the very soft sounds inside your body?

Here is another help to
hearing. It is an electric
hearing aid. It uses electricity to make sounds
louder.

What does the doctor see when he looks into
your ear?

He sees a little sheet of skin called an eardrum. Your eardrums are very important parts of your ears. Let's see what they do. Let's build a tin-can eardrum.

EXPERIMENT

You will need a tin can with both ends cut out, a rubber balloon, a rubber band, and some dry cereal. Stretch the balloon rubber across one end of the can. Fasten it with a rubber band. Put three or four pieces of dry cereal across the stretched rubber.

Now ask somebody to say "boom-boom-boom" from underneath. What happens to the cereal? What do sound vibrations do to the stretched rubber?

The sheet of rubber is like the eardrum in your ear. Sound vibrations make the eardrum vibrate. The eardrum sends vibrations inside, and then you hear. What would happen if the eardrum were broken? Can you tell why you must NEVER put a sharp-pointed or hard thing into your ear?

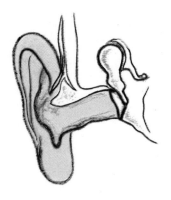

Listen! Listen to the sounds around you. Think of all the sounds you hear every day — sounds of music, sounds of talking, sounds of animals. So much of the world comes to you through sound!

THINGS TO TALK ABOUT

1. Talk about the sounds you hear on your way to school. Can you tell what made each sound?

2. Talk about sounds you like to hear.

3. Talk about how important sound is in our everyday lives.

4. Tell why you must take good care of your ears. What are some good rules to remember about the care of your ears?

5. Talk about the different sounds that animals make. How do they make the sounds?

THINGS TO DO

1. Make a musical scale. Pour a little water into a drinking glass. Strike it gently with a pencil and listen to the sound that it makes. Pour a little more water into the second glass. Strike it with a pencil and try to hear if the sound is different. Pour different amounts of water into six more glasses. Try to fix them so that the sounds they make will form a scale.

2. Look at the inside of a piano. Are all the strings alike? Strike the notes. Watch what happens inside the piano. Where do the high sounds come from? Where do the low sounds come from?

3. Bring in some musical toys. Tell what makes the sound in each.

4. Get different kinds of coins. Drop each coin on a hard table top. Listen to the sounds the coins make. Close your eyes. Have someone else drop the coins. Can you tell what coin it is by the sound it makes?

5. Fold a piece of very thin paper in half and put a comb into it. Hum a tune while your lips touch the paper. What can you feel with your lips?

THINGS TO FIND OUT

1. Not all animals have ears that can be seen. Find out where the ears of these animals are.

2. Find out how the ears of a bat help it to find its way.

3. Find out why sounds seem louder in an empty room.

WE USE ELECTRICITY

In this kitchen electricity is being used in many ways. Electricity is making light in the electric lamps. It is making heat in the electric iron, the electric toaster, the waffle iron, and the range. It is turning the hands of the clock and the blades of the mixer.

The same kind of electricity can do three kinds of things for us. It can make light, it can make heat, or it can make something move. Let's see how electricity does these three things for us.

Electricity Makes Light

EXPERIMENT

You will need a thin piece of wire. You can get this by pulling out one piece from a picture wire or from an old piece of electric wire.

You will also need a dry cell to give the electricity for your experiment. The electricity from a dry cell is safe to use. But electricity in your house wires can hurt you badly if you try to do experiments with it.

Hold the wire by its two ends and place it across the two screws of the dry cell.

Watch the wire between the two screws begin to glow. When electricity goes through a thin wire that is made of the right material, the wire becomes red hot and glows. It gives off light.

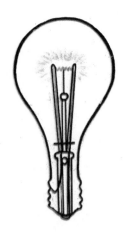

Look at this picture of an electric light bulb. You can see that it has a thin wire inside. When the electricity goes through this thin wire, the wire glows and gives off light.

Electricity makes light for many different uses. What can you tell about each of these lights?

Electricity Makes Heat

You have seen that electricity can make the thin wire in a bulb give off light. The wire also gives off heat, even though we do not need heat from a bulb. But in a toaster or electric iron we want as much heat as possible. How can we get more heat and less light from the electricity?

E X P E R I M E N T

Get a thick piece of picture wire and hold it by its two ends. Place it across the two screws of the dry cell.

Does it glow as brightly as the thin wire?

Ask somebody to hold a small piece of paper near the wire. Does the paper begin to smoke? It is the heat from the wire that makes the paper so hot.

When enough electricity flows through a wire, we get light and heat. If the wire is thin enough, we get more light than heat. If the wire is thicker, we get more heat than light. There are thick wires in electric toasters, heaters, irons, and ranges. You can easily see the wires in electric heaters and toasters.

Electricity Moves Things

Electricity can move things. Electricity moves the hands of an electric clock. It moves the machinery in a vacuum cleaner, in an electric fan, in an electric train, and in many other things. In your school gong, electricity moves a little hammer that hits the gong and makes it ring. Let's see how electricity can make things move. Let's make a small gong.

EXPERIMENT

You will need a glass jar, some thread, a pencil, a large iron nail, a dry cell, an iron screw or nut, and about five feet of covered wire.

Wrap the wire around the iron nail, as in the picture. Cut away the covering from each end of the wire. Bend each end into a little hook.

Now you have a special kind of magnet, called an electromagnet. It can pull things made of iron. To see how it works, let's use it to make the gong.

Put the electromagnet inside the jar. Tie the iron screw or nut to the end of the pencil and lay the pencil across the top of the jar.

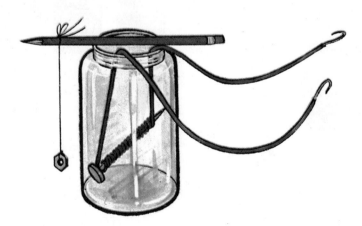

Hook one end of the electromagnet wire onto one screw of the dry cell. Then tap the other end against the other screw. Tap, take away, tap, take away. What happens? How is the sound made?

Here is a school gong. How many electromagnets does it have? Where is the part that strikes the gong? What makes this part move?

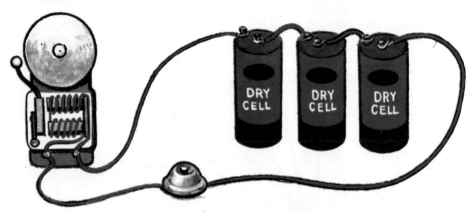

You have seen how electromagnets can make something move back and forth. They can also make something move around and around.

In an electric motor there are electromagnets that make an iron wheel spin around. The spinning iron wheel then turns the blades of a fan, or the hands of a clock, or other machines that run by electricity.

Each one of these machines has an electric motor inside. Can you tell what each electric motor does?

Electricity Stops and Goes

You have seen how electricity can make a thin wire glow and give off light. But the thin wire in a bulb is way inside. How do we bring electricity to it? Perhaps this picture will help you to remember.

You needed two wires to make the bulb light up because the electricity had to flow all the way around. It flowed out of one part of the dry cell, through one wire, into the bulb. Then it flowed through the second wire, back into another part of the dry cell.

Now you have joined the bulb and a dry cell so that the bulb lights up. But how can you make the light go out? You could do it by taking away one of the wires. But that is not how you turn off the lights in your house.

You use a switch. Let's see how it works.

EXPERIMENT

You will need a dry cell, three pieces of covered wire, a small lamp socket, a flashlight bulb, a small block of wood, two thumbtacks with metal heads, and an aluminum food container such as a pie tin.

Cut a strip of aluminum about three inches long and an inch wide from the container. Cut off the covering from the ends of the wire.

Push a thumbtack through the aluminum strip and part way into the wood. Then push another thumbtack part way into the wood, about two inches away.

Now join the wires as in the picture and push the thumbtacks all the way in.

Push the strip of aluminum against the thumbtack. Does the bulb light? Then lift it up. What happens now? Move the strip up and down. Watch the light go off and on.

You have made an electric switch.

Aluminum is a metal. The thumbtacks and electric wires are made of metal, too. Electricity can flow through metal.

When you touch the end of the aluminum strip to the thumbtack, electricity flows through the thumbtacks, the strip, and the wires.

The electricity flows in a complete metal path from the dry cell to the bulb and back to another part of the dry cell.

When you lift the strip you break the path. Electricity can not flow across the open space, and the bulb stops shining. A real switch has a metal strip too, and it works in almost the same way.

There is a metal strip inside. When you snap a button or pull a chain on the switch, the metal strip is moved into place. With the strip in place, we have a complete metal path. Electricity can flow and light the bulb.

When you snap the button again, or pull the chain again, the metal strip is moved away. The electricity cannot flow across the open space, and the bulb goes out.

You can use the things you learned about bulbs and switches in this way. You can help make a place in which to give plays.

THINGS TO TALK ABOUT

1. Talk about things in your home which give heat from electricity.

2. Tell why you should NEVER do experiments with the electricity from house wires. What may you use? What safety rules must be followed in doing experiments with electricity?

3. Talk about how electricity saves work for your mother.

4. Talk about things that run by electricity from dry cells.

5. Tell how electricity is used on a farm.

6. Tell how homes were lighted before there were electric lamps.

THINGS TO DO

1. Bring in toys that run by electricity. Tell how they work.

2. Make an electromagnet like the one on page 271. Try to find out what materials the electromagnet will pick up.

3. Visit the basement of your school. Ask to be shown the electric wires and switches. You may also want to be shown some of the large electric motors. Ask to see the machines by which the electric company

finds out how much electricity is used. Watch them for a little while.

4. Make a bell ring. Use a dry cell, wire, and an electric bell. Join the wire so that you have a closed path. Try to see how the electromagnet in the bell makes the bell ring.

THINGS TO FIND OUT

1. How can you tell how much light a lamp bulb will give out? Find out.

2. Find out some uses of dry cells. Are dry cells all alike? Try to bring some used dry cells to show your class.

3. Find out how many different things in a car run by electricity.

4. Find out how traffic lights change color.

5. Find out where the main switch in your house is. Why is it important to know where it is?

6. Find out how many different kinds of switches there are in your home. How many can you see in school?

READABILITY ANALYSIS

Science Far and Near, the third book in the HEATH SCIENCE SERIES, meets the requirements of third grade readability.

The Spache Readability Formula for Primary Grades was used to evaluate the over-all readability of the book. This formula reveals that *Science Far and Near* has a grade placement of 2.7, the level of a second reader, which clearly indicates that the book is well within the reading ability of third grade children.

The total vocabulary of *Science Far and Near* is 1242 words. Of these, 1017 words are assumed to be known by third grade children because they were introduced in the first and second grade books of this series, or because they were rated by Gates' revised *Reading Vocabulary for the Primary Grades* as "highly suitable for use in all forms of reading material in grades 1, 2, and 3 — especially grades 1 and 2." Variants are counted as new words except for variants formed by adding the endings *s, 's, s', es, d, ed, r, er, est, ly, y, n, en, ing,* and *ful;* or by doubling the final consonant, dropping the final *e,* or changing the final *y* to *i* before adding any of these endings. A compound word formed by combining two known words is not considered a new word; nor is a part of a known compound when used alone. In addition, 16 words of the total vocabulary are presented in vocabulary enrichment exercises on the activity pages at the ends of the units and are therefore not considered part of the readability study.

The 209 new words used in *Science Far and Near* are introduced gradually. Of the 278 pages in the book that contain text material, 150 pages introduce no new words at all; and 98% of the remaining 128 pages introduce 3 or fewer new words per page. The average rate of introduction of new words is .75 new words per page, or one new word per 126 running words. The average number of repetitions per new word is 5.8.

Of the 2595 sentences in the book, 96% contain 18 or fewer words. The average sentence length is 10.2 words.

The amount of text on each page has been carefully controlled, so that there is an average of one illustration for every 72 running words.

The 209 new words in *Science Far and Near* are presented on the following pages. The numbers refer to the pages on which the words first occur.